FABULOUS ITALIAN RECIPES

by

Johna Blinn

Edited by
Tom Dorsey

PUBLISHED BY PLAYMORE INC., PUBLISHERS AND WALDMAN PUBLISHING CORP.
New York, New York
Printed in Canada

Fabulous Cookbook Series
Prepared Under the Editorial Direction of
Malvina G. Vogel

Illustrated by Arthur Friedman

Designed by Irva Mandelbaum

Cover photo: Lasagna Verdi
Courtesy of Campbell Soup Company

To Caryl & Marilyn

Acknowledgments:

This writer is especially indebted to the expert advice, encouragement and cooperation of many. I am particularly indebted to Ruth Lundgren, Olive Dempsey, Chris Pines, Caryl Saunders, Claire Boasi, Anita Fial, Pat Mason, A.C. Collins, Marilyn Kaytor, Ed Justin, The Fresh Garlic Association, Lea & Perrins Worcestershire Sauce, American Mushroom Association, Tuna Research Foundation, McIlhenny Co., Anita Mizner, Howard Helmer, Prince Foods Light Pasta, Barbara Robinson, Sunkist Growers, Inc., California Milk Advisory Board, American Egg Board, Florida Celery Committee, California Iceberg Lettuce Commission, American Dairy Association, American Spice Trade Association, Virginia Schroeder, Alice Gautsch, Eileen Edwards Denne, Borden's Lite-Line Pasteurized Process Cheese Product, Quaker Oats Co., Carolyn Coughlin, California Fresh Market Tomato Advisory Board, Margaret Spader, Fleischmann's (unsalted margarine and 100% corn oil margarine), Florida Citrus Commission, National Broiler Council, Idaho Potato Commission, California Table Grape Commission, Campbell Soup Co., Angostura International Limited, Rice Council, Rae Hartfield, Betsy Slinkard, Argo and Kingsford's Corn Starch, United Fresh Fruit and Vegetable Association, Gloria Marshall, Marilyn Dompe, National Fisheries Institute, Inc., Patricia O'Keefe, California Artichoke Advisory Board, Mazola Corn Oil, Castle & Cooke Foods (Dole/Bumble Bee), Virginia Pinegreen, Donna Higgins, Del Monte Kitchens, Dot Tringali, Kay Murphy O'Flynn, Washington State Apple Commission, Dee Munson, Lois Westlund, Egg Beaters Cholesterol-free Egg Substitute, California Avocado Commission, Charcoal Briquet Institute, Alaska Seafood Marketing Institute, Washington State Potato Commission, Hellmann's and Best Foods Mayonnaise, Roxie Howlett, Diamond Walnut Kitchen, Skippy Peanut Butter, Karo Corn Syrup, Planter's Peanut Oil Test Kitchen, Standard Brands, Inc., National Turkey Federation, Christine Dozel, Jan Kerman, South African Rock Lobster Service Corporation, Nucoa Margarine, Diane Cline, Frances Fleming, Virginia Schroeder, Lawry's Ltd., California Milk Advisory Board, Ray Clark, National Duckling Council, California Bartlett Growers, Inc., O'Neal F. Caliendo, Yvonne Martin, National Capon Council, National Goose Council, National Livestock and Meat Board, American Lamb Council, Olive Administrative Committee, Fleischmann's Active Dry Yeast, Blue Bonnet Margarine, California Dried Fig Advisory Board, Beef Industry Council, Peanut Advisory Board, National Pork Producers Council, Kikkoman International Inc., New Zealand Lamb Co., Jan Works, Schiling Division McCormick and Co., National Cherry Growers & Industries Foundation, Susan Martinson, Jan Sirochman, Golden Grain Macaroni Co., Sweet Potato Council of California, Donna Hamilton, B.J. McCabe, Leafy Greens Council, Marcia L. Watts, California Turkey Industry Board, Frani Lauda, Italian Wine Center, National Macaroni Institute, J. Marsiglia, California Almond Growers Exchange, Bertolli's (olive oil, red-Italian wine vinegar, spaghetti sauce and wines), North American Blueberry Council, Fenella Pearson, Florio (dry and sweet Marsala wines), Ken Bray, 21 Brands (Liquore Galliano), Sherrie Newman, Wyler's Beef-Flavored Instant Bouillon, Jamaica Resort Hotels, Borden Company, Los Angeles Smoking and Curing Company, Mrs. Cubbison's Foods, Inc., Catherine Stratemeyer, Southern Belle English Walnuts, Denmark Cheese Association, Shirley Mack, Beans of the West, International Multifoods (Kretschmer Wheat Germ) and Imported Winter Grapes Association.

J.B.

BARONET
B·O·O·K·S

BARONET BOOKS is a trademark of Playmore Inc., Publishers
and Waldman Publishing Corp., New York, N.Y.

The Author

To many of the top movie and television stars, Johna Blinn is a celebrity. For almost 20 years they have welcomed her into their homes, onto sets, just about anywhere to talk about food, entertaining and lifestyles. Her column, "Celebrity Cookbook," is syndicated throughout the world and appears weekly in more than 140 newspapers and periodicals. A collection of hundreds of these conversations and recipes appears in *Celebrity Cookbook*, published by Waldman Publishing Corporation.

Blinn is a former assistant food editor of LOOK magazine and is the author of a number of books, including *The Shangri-la Cookbook*. While she is busy working on her first novel and screenplay, Blinn still manages to serve as a frequent contributor of indepth interviews, profiles and entertainment features to newspapers and magazines in the U. S. and abroad.

A graduate of the State University of Iowa, Blinn took graduate work in home economics at the University of Wisconsin and taught home economics in Iowa, Virginia and New York. Now based in Los Angeles, she is married to a nationally-known newspaper syndicate editor, writer and management consultant, and they have two teenage children.

Introduction

Like no other people in the world, Italians probably know more about how to cook and eat than almost any other people on the face of the earth! Their attitudes toward food also reflect in their approach to life. Typically, they spend long, leisurely hours over lunch or dinner in trattorie or ristoranti, because to them, eating and dining is one of the great pleasures in life.

The hallmarks of Italian cooking are simple, uncomplicated recipes handed down from mother to daughter. Italian housewives shop daily to obtain the finest and freshest of produce and ingredients. And as more and more Americans travel to Italian shores, they are discovering that the traditional fare — antipasto, minestrone, spaghetti, veal scaloppini and spumoni—served in most Italian-American restaurants, is only a small part of Italian dishes.

Because Italy stretches over a 600-mile area from north to south, it is natural that there should be variation in foods and drinks served from region to region. For example, people in northern Italy feel that their eating habits have little in common with those of the South. Northern Italians are rice lovers; Southern Italians, passionate pasta lovers. Northern Italians are famous for their risotto alla milanese — a rice dish flavored with saffron or minestrone, a thick vegetable soup. Venetians are fond of rice combined with green peas — risi-bisi, as it is called — and rice combined with sausage or shellfish.

Venetians are blessed by the Adriatic Sea and rely on a quantity of fish, as do most Italians, especially those who live along the coasts. Scampi is a Venetian favorite. Farther south along the Mediterranean, calamares (squid) are a popular staple.

Around Rome, where mild-flavored dishes are more common than the highly aromatic, garlic-flavored dishes of their Sicilian neighbors, Romans are addicted to fettuccine — the golden noodles served with freshly grated cheese and/or Prosciutto ham. And how they love their vegetables: carciofi (artichokes fried in boiling olive oil) and fritto misto, a fried mix usually made with cauliflower, cheese, green pepper, mushrooms, and cubed chicken or veal, all batter-dipped and cooked quickly in olive oil until golden!

The rich Sicilian soil plus the Mediterranean Sea combine to give the people of Sicily an infinite variety of tempting taste treats. Sardines, swordfish and shellfish are only a few of the plentiful but popular fish or seafood. Sicilians love to fry, stuff, batter-fry, and casserole the eggplant, while satisfying their sweet tooth with the profusion of fruits, nuts, cakes, cream puffs, and candy.

In Sardinia, polenta (a cornmeal mush) is eaten more often than in other provinces. Many gnocchi (dumplings) — made from farina, semolina, cornmeal, and white flour — find their way into soup served as a main dish with tomato sauce and cheese or as a side dish to accompany meat. Sardinia is also the home of many wild game dishes, including hare, wild duck, woodcock, and quail. Travelers never forget the local lamb or kid roasted on a spit, over sweet-smelling wood.

In Naples, pizza (closed or fried) and veal scaloppini are as popular with the natives as they are with visitors.

Although only a few of the culinary wonders of Italy have been mentioned, one feature is common to all Italians — a love and respect for good food. Breakfast is usually brief: a hunk of bread or a roll, served with coffee. Lunch never lasts less than two hours. A typical luncheon menu includes an antipasto (choice of marinated vegetables, seafood, eggs, cheese, olives, or sausages) or soup, followed by a choice of pasta, rice, or gnocchi. The main event stars fish, meat or chicken with a fresh vegetable in season and a green salad. A choice of fruits and cheeses usually concludes the meal. Sweet desserts (dolci) are reserved for festive occasions. Dinner is eaten late and is usually a more elaborate version of the luncheon menu, always served with wines. The main meal is never complete without coffee espresso or one of its variations, such as cappuccino.

Italian cooking is not difficult once you familiarize yourself with its staples: tomato, garlic, herbs, olive oil, cheeses, vegetables, and pasta. Preparing an Italian meal can be a rewarding experience, especially if you are looking for new ideas without straining your budget. For example, the healthy Italian habit of eating many greens makes salad-making as easy as picking your own dandelion greens or choosing less familiar greens such as chicory, escarole, and romaine. Italians excel at cooking vegetables, such as creating culinary delights from zucchini, eggplant, and cauliflower. Discovering new kinds of pasta can be adventuresome. A special recipe section of pasta with off-beat sauces, ranging from pesto to the familiar Bolognese, is included.

Economy is an important factor that makes Italian-style cooking attractive to Americans. Italians traditionally consume less meat than Americans, relying on eggs, cheese, fish, and fowl to provided the needed protein. The recipes that follow are for easy but inexpensive Italian culinary creations that won't send you scouring the supermarket or gourmet shops, but that will earn you rave notices from family and friends.

J.B.

CONTENTS

Assorted Italian Hors d'Oeuvres

Prosciutto, thinly sliced, served with melon (plain or lightly sprinkled with ginger or well-soaked in wine). To do this, cut a small round off the top of melon, scoop out and discard seeds. Pour glass of Marsala wine or sherry into melon. Chill until almost frozen. To serve, cut into small cubes with prosciutto.

Cut about ¼ pound firm cheese (Bel Paese or similar cheese) into cubes. Remove pits from 1 dozen ripe black olives. Fry cheese and olives together in butter until cheese blisters. Add 1 teaspoon dry white wine and simmer 2 minutes. Serve on hot buttered toast. Sprinkle with freshly grated black pepper.

Arrange assorted cold meats and sausages on a platter. These can include cold beef (cooked very rare), lamb, ham, pork and veal. Include sausage (the spicier, the better) and cheese. (Italians like to eat small bites as a prelude to the main meal.)

Artichokes Italian

Serves 6

6 medium artichokes
1½ cups olive or salad oil
½ cup white wine vinegar
¼ cup water
1 tablespoon salt
1 teaspoon sugar
¾ teaspoon oregano, crushed
¾ teaspoon basil, crushed
¼ teaspoon dry mustard
¼ teaspoon pepper
1 large clove garlic
½ pound cauliflower, cut into
  small flowerets

¼ pound mushrooms, sliced
1 cup sliced carrots, about
  2 medium
½ cup pitted ripe olives,
  cut into slivers
½ cup Italian salami, cut into
  strips (about ⅛ pound)
½ cup diced Fontina or Provolone
  cheese (about ⅛ pound)
¼ cup whole pimientos, drained
  and diced
1 can (7 ounces) water-pack tuna,
  drained

1. Prepare artichokes according to directions on page 72. Set aside.
2. Combine oil, wine vinegar, water, salt, sugar, oregano, basil, dry mustard, pepper and garlic in saucepan.
3. Heat to boiling; boil gently 5 minutes.
4. Add cauliflower, mushrooms and carrots; heat to boiling.
5. Simmer gently 3 to 5 minutes, or until vegetables are crisp-tender.
6. Chill in liquid.
7. Drain vegetables, reserving liquid for marinade.
8. Combine drained, chilled vegetables with olives, salami, cheese, and pimientos in large bowl.
9. Toss tuna into antipasto mixture, keeping pieces as whole as possible.
10. To serve, spoon some antipasto mixture into each prepared chilled artichoke, spreading artichoke leaves to hold filling.
11. Serve reserved marinade for dipping artichoke leaves, stirring marinade frequently.

Pickled Artichokes

Serves 4 to 6

1 package (9 ounces) frozen
   artichoke hearts
2 tablespoons peanut oil
1 tablespoon white vinegar
¼ teaspoon salt

¼ teaspoon sugar
¼ teaspoon oregano leaves
¼ teaspoon prepared mustard
⅛ teaspoon pepper
1 bay leaf
1 clove garlic

1. Cook frozen artichoke hearts according to package directions; drain.
2. Combine peanut oil with remaining ingredients in bowl; stir in artichoke hearts.
3. Cover tightly and refrigerate until well chilled, turning artichoke hearts occasionally in marinade.

NOTE: Pickled artichokes are popular as a first course.

Marinated Artichoke Hearts & Mushrooms

Serves 4

1 jar (6 ounces) marinated
   artichoke hearts
½ pound fresh whole mushrooms,
   cleaned

½ cup homemade or top-quality bottled
   Italian dressing
2 tablespoons fresh, snipped
   parsley or dill

1. Empty artichokes and liquid into bowl.
2. Add whole mushrooms and Italian dressing; toss until mushrooms are coated.
3. Turn into container and sprinkle with herbs.
4. Serve cold as antipasto.

Antipasto Toss

Serves 6 to 8

1 medium head lettuce, torn in
   small pieces
½ pound cooked beef, cut in
   strips (about 1½ cups)
½ pound salami, cut in
   strips (2 cups)
¼ pound Gorgonzola cheese
   or blue cheese, crumbled (1 cup)

¼ pound fresh mush-
   rooms, sliced (1 cup)
1 small green pepper, cut in
   strips
½ cup pimiento-stuffed or
   ripe olives
1 bottle (8 ounces) Italian-
   style dressing

carrot curls and parsley (optional garnish)

1. Toss all ingredients with dressing in large salad bowl.
2. If desired, garnish with carrot curls and parsley.

Caponata

Makes 4½ cups

2 pounds eggplant (2 small)
2 cups chopped onion
2 cups diced, peeled tomatoes
  (3 medium)
1 cup chopped celery
¼ cup olive oil
1 small clove garlic, minced

1 can (11 ounces) condensed tomato
  bisque soup
¼ cup wine vinegar
¼ cup water
½ cup pitted ripe olives, sliced
2 tablespoons sugar
2 tablespoons pine nuts, chopped

1. Peel eggplants; cut in ½-inch cubes.
2. Cook eggplant in boiling salted water in saucepan 10 minutes; drain well.
3. Meanwhile, cook onion, tomatoes and celery in olive oil in skillet until tender.
4. Add eggplant and remaining ingredients. Cook over low heat 10 minutes, stirring occasionally.
5. Chill 6 hours or more.

NOTE: This thick vegetable relish is an antipasto or first course. It should be served chilled on lettuce leaves or with crusty bread.

Antipasto

Serves 6 to 8

1 can (10¾ ounces) condensed
  tomato soup
½ cup olive oil
½ cup red wine vinegar
1 package (6 ounce) mild Italian
  salad dressing mix

2 cups diagonally sliced carrots
2 cups small cauliflowerets
2 cups cubed zucchini squash
2 cups small fresh mushroom caps
½ cup pimiento-stuffed olives
1 medium green pepper, cut in strips

½ cup sliced pepperoni

1. Combine soup, oil, vinegar and salad dressing mix in small saucepan. Bring to boil.
2. Reduce heat and simmer 5 minutes, stirring occasionally.
3. Arrange vegetables and pepperoni in shallow dish.
4. Pour marinade over vegetable-pepperoni mixture.
5. Chill 6 hours or more, stirring occasionally.
6. Serve with slotted spoon.

Formaggio

Makes 5 dozen hors d'oeuvres

½ cup milk
2 eggs, slightly beaten
1½ cups fine dry bread crumbs
⅛ teaspoon salt

⅛ teaspoon pepper
1 pound Bel Paese cheese, cut in
  bite-size pieces
peanut oil

1. Combine milk and eggs; set aside.
2. Mix together bread crumbs, salt and pepper.
3. Dip cheese pieces in milk/egg mixture, then coat with seasoned bread crumbs. Repeat.
4. Fry in oil heated to 375° F., or until golden.
5. Remove from fryer and drain on paper towels. Serve immediately.

Mushrooms Antipasto

Makes 2 quarts

3 pounds fresh mushrooms
2 cups water
2 cups thinly sliced celery
1 tablespoon chopped parsley
1 can (9 ounces) pitted black
  olives, drained and sliced

1 jar (8 ounces) stuffed green
  olives, drained and sliced
2 large cloves garlic, mashed
1½ teaspoons ground black pepper
½ cup olive oil
¼ cup white vinegar

1. Rinse, pat dry, and slice mushrooms (makes about 15 cups).
2. Put water in large saucepan; heat to boiling point.
3. Add mushrooms; cover and simmer 5 minutes.
4. Drain and rinse quickly with cold water; dry with paper towels.
5. Place mushrooms in large mixing bowl. Add remaining ingredients and toss gently.
6. Cover and chill thoroughly.
7. Serve as a salad in lettuce cups, if desired, or as an hors d' oeuvre.

Prosciutto e Melone
(Prosciutto & Melon)

Serves 4

1 ripe cantaloupe
½ pound very thinly sliced
  prosciutto

2 or 3 ripe olives (optional
  garnish)
freshly ground black pepper

1. Cut top and bottom off melon. Cut in half and scoop out seeds.
2. Cut each half lengthwise into 4 slices. Trim away all skin and green-tinged flesh, leaving only ripe melon.
3. Cover and chill, if necessary.
4. At serving time, arrange 3 or 4 slices of prosciutto on individual salad plates with a garnish of 2 slices of melon. Or arrange a serving platter with prosciutto in center and melon slices arranged petal fashion around outer edge.
5. If desired, garnish with 2 or 3 ripe olives. Let guests use pepper mill over prosciutto.

Italian Bread & Tuna Soup

Serves 8

2 cans (7 ounces each) tuna,
    packed in oil
1 cup chopped onion
2 large cloves garlic, pressed
1 can (8 ounces) tomatoes, drained
    and chopped

6 slices Italian bread, cubed
8 cups clear vegetable broth
    (made with vegetable bouillon
    cubes and water)
minced fresh parsley (for garnish)
hard-cooked egg (for garnish)

1. Drain 3 tablespoons oil from tuna into large stockpot; heat oil.
2. Sauté onion and garlic in oil until soft.
3. Add tomatoes; cook 2 minutes.
4. Add bread cubes and cook 2 minutes longer.
5. Stir in broth and tuna; simmer 30 minutes.
6. Serve piping hot, garnished with minced parsley and hard-cooked egg.

Tony's Zuppa Contadina
(Peasant Soup)

Serves 6

1 small onion, peeled
1 stalk celery
1 carrot, peeled
1 clove garlic, peeled
3 cups chopped fresh parsley
½ cup olive oil
1 pound fresh shelled lima beans

5 cups hot water
1½ teaspoons salt
freshly ground black pepper
1 pound fresh Swiss chard
6 slices day-old Italian bread,
    toasted or fried in olive oil
    (optional)

1. Chop together onion, celery, carrot, garlic and parsley until very fine.
2. Sauté in olive oil in soup kettle until colors start to change.
3. Add shelled lima beans to vegetable-herb mixture.
4. Add water, salt and pepper; bring to a boil.
5. Lower heat and cook 20 minutes, or until beans are almost tender.
6. Wash chard thoroughly three times; trim stalks of coarse ribs and chop into ½-inch bits.
7. When beans are almost cooked, add chard.
8. Raise heat and continue cooking 10 minutes longer, or until chard stems are tender.
9. Taste to correct seasonings.
10. Serve one slice of Italian bread in bottom of each soup plate. Spoon soup over it.

Zuppa di Clams

Serves 2

12 unshucked clams
2 small cloves garlic, minced
2 tablespoons olive oil
4 cups clam juice
1 cup drained canned tomatoes, puréed

salt to taste
white pepper to taste
⅛ teaspoon oregano
⅛ teaspoon basil
2 tablespoons minced parsley
Italian bread

1. Wash and scrub clams well.
2. Sauté garlic in olive oil in saucepan.
3. Add clams, clam juice and tomatoes; season to taste with salt and white pepper.
4. Add oregano, basil and parsley.
5. Cover and cook over low heat until shells open.
6. Spoon into shallow soup bowls.
7. Serve with crusty Italian bread. It's great and low in calories too!

Pallottoline in Brodo
(Meatballs in Soup)

Serves 4 to 6

2 cans (10½ ounces each) condensed chicken with rice soup
1½ soup cans water
⅓ cup chopped onion
¼ cup chopped carrot
¼ cup chopped celery
1 large clove garlic, minced
2 tablespoons chopped parsley
½ teaspoon salt (optional)

½ pound lean ground beef (ground twice)
3 tablespoons grated Parmesan or Romano cheese
2 tablespoons fine bread crumbs
1 egg, slightly beaten
⅛ teaspoon freshly ground black pepper
2 to 3 tablespoons flour

1 cup chopped fresh tomatoes

1. Combine soup, water, onion, carrot, celery, garlic, parsley and salt in large saucepan. Bring to boil.
2. Reduce heat and simmer 30 minutes, stirring occasionally.
3. Meanwhile, combine beef, cheese, bread crumbs, egg and pepper in mixing bowl.
4. Shape into 48 small meatballs. Dust meatballs with flour.
5. Add meatballs and tomatoes to simmering soup. Simmer 10 minutes longer, or until done.

NOTE: The fact that the meatballs are poached in the soup makes it unusual. Serve as first or main course.

Italian Pasta Pot

Serves 6 to 8

½ cup chopped green pepper
1 large clove garlic, minced
¼ teaspoon rosemary leaves, crushed
2 tablespoons olive oil
3 cans (10¾ ounces each) tomato soup
3 soup cans water

1 can (16 ounces) chick peas, drained
1 cup cooked small-shell macaroni
2 teaspoons anchovy fillets, chopped
freshly grated Parmesan cheese (optional garnish)

1. Cook green pepper, garlic and rosemary in olive oil in large saucepan.
2. Stir in soup and water.
3. Add remaining ingredients except cheese, stirring occasionally.
4. Garnish with grated Parmesan cheese, if desired.

Zuppa di Pesce
(Fish Soup)

Serves 4

2 tablespoons olive oil
1 clove garlic, minced
1 onion, peeled and chopped
1 tablespoon chopped parsley

2 cups cold water
1½ pounds whitefish fillets, cut in 2-inch pieces
salt to taste
pepper to taste

1. Heat oil in heavy pot. Add garlic, onion and parsley; sauté until onion softens.
2. Add water, fish, salt and pepper; bring to boil.
3. Immediately lower heat to simmer; cook 10 minutes, or until fish is cooked.
4. Serve hot with Italian bread and butter.

Red Sea Clam Chowder

Serves 6

6 slices bacon, diced
½ cup chopped onion
1 cup chopped celery
1 clove garlic, minced
1 can (28 ounces) tomatoes
1 cup water

1 can (12 ounces) tomato vegetable juice
1 teaspoon salt
⅛ teaspoon freshly ground black pepper
2 cups large shell macaroni
2 cans (6½ ounces each) chopped clams
¼ cup minced parsley

1. Sauté bacon 5 minutes. Add onion, celery, and garlic; cook until bacon is brown.
2. Pour off most of the excess fat.
3. Add tomatoes, water, vegetable juice, salt and pepper. Bring to boil.
4. Stir in shell macaroni, cover, and cook 12 minutes, stirring once.
5. Add clams and parsley and simmer 5 minutes.

Minestrone

Serves 8 to 10

3 slices lean bacon, minced
1 cup chopped onion
½ cup chopped celery
2 large cloves garlic, minced
1 teaspoon basil leaves, crushed
1 can (10½ ounces) condensed
  beef broth
1 can (11½ ounces) condensed bean
  with bacon soup

1½ soup cans water
1 can (16 ounces) tomatoes,
  undrained
½ cup uncooked ditalini
  (small tube macaroni)
½ teaspoon salt
1 cup cabbage, cut in long
  thin shreds
1 cup cubed zucchini squash

1. Brown bacon in large skillet; pour off and discard most of fat.
2. Add onion, celery, garlic and basil in skillet; cook until vegetables are tender.
3. Stir in soups, water, tomatoes, ditalini and salt. Bring to boil.
4. Reduce heat, cover and simmer 15 minutes.
5. Add cabbage and zucchini; cook 10 minutes longer, or until tender, stirring occasionally.

Zuppa di Carciofi
(Artichoke Soup)

Serves 6

⅔ cup chopped onion
2 medium cloves garlic, minced
1 teaspoon thyme leaves, crushed
generous dash white pepper
¼ cup olive oil
2 cans (10¾ cups each) condensed
  chicken broth
1 cup water
¼ cup dry white wine

2 packages (9 ounces each) frozen
  artichoke hearts, thawed and
  drained
1 cup diced potato
2 bay leaves
1 cup heavy cream
3 tablespoons grated Parmesan cheese
2 tablespoons butter
2 small tomatoes, chopped (for garnish)

1. Cook onion with garlic, thyme and pepper in olive oil in large saucepan until tender.
2. Add broth, water, wine, artichoke hearts, potato and bay leaves. Bring to boil.
3. Reduce heat and simmer 20 minutes, or until done.
4. Remove any bay leaves.
5. Blend soup mixture in electric blender, a little at a time, until smooth.
6. Return mixture to saucepan. Gradually stir in remaining ingredients.
7. Garnish with cooked quartered artichokes and chopped tomato.

Zuppa di Pesce Alla Siciliana
(Sicilian Fish Soup)

Serves 8

2 pounds unboned fish: about ½ pound
  each whiting, red snapper, sea bass
  and porgy shells from ½ pound shrimp
  (reserve shrimp)
1½ quarts water
6 chopped tomatoes
3 cloves garlic, chopped
3 teaspoons salt
½ teaspoon freshly ground
  black pepper

½ pound diced squid or scallops
1 tablespoon olive oil
4 leeks, cut into 1½-inch strips
1 tablespoon butter
pinch saffron
¾ cup dry white wine
3 tablespoons heavy cream
1 cup cooked vermicelli
Rust Sauce (optional)
grated Parmesan cheese (optional)
Italian bread (optional)

1. Place fish and shrimp shells in large stockpot.
2. Add 1 quart water, 3 chopped tomatoes, garlic, 1 teaspoon salt and ¼ teaspoon pepper.
3. Cover and simmer 30 minutes.
4. Strain and reserve stock. Discard fish fragments.
5. Cut reserved shrimp into small pieces and cook briefly with squid in olive oil.
6. Season with salt and pepper to taste; set aside.
7. Place leeks and butter in skillet; brown leeks.
8. Add to skillet remaining tomatoes, saffron, wine, remaining water, reserved fish stock, remaining salt and remaining pepper.
9. Cover and simmer 30 minutes.
10. Add squid and shrimp; mix.
11. Stir in cream and vermicelli; heat gently.
12. Serve with Rust Sauce, if desired (1 teaspoon or so per serving), a side dish of grated Parmesan cheese and Italian bread slices fried in garlic butter. Bread can be served separately or added to soup, topped with cheese.

Rust Sauce

6 cloves garlic
4 pimientos
2 egg yolks
8 drops Tabasco sauce

salt to taste
pepper to taste
¼ cup olive oil
2 tablespoons hot soup

1. Blend garlic, pimientos, egg yolks, Tabasco, salt and pepper in blender.
2. Add olive oil, drop by drop, and blend until smooth.
3. Stir in hot soup.
4. Serve as a side dish or stir into soup.

About Pasta, Risotto & Gnocchi

More than any country in the world, Italy has an incredible variety of macaroni products in an amazing number of forms, shapes and sizes. There are numerous legends about the origin of the pasta products. Some claim that a Chinese maiden taught her Italian sailor sweetheart the art of noodle-making — an art which he brought back to his native land. This parallels the myth that Marco Polo is supposed to have returned to his native Venice with gunpowder, coal and noodles from the court of the Great Khan of Tartary.

Another legend tells that a wealthy nobleman of Palermo — possibly a thirteenth-century king — who was noted for his love of find food, possessed a cook with a marvelously inventive genuis. One day this talented cook devised the farinaceous tubes with which we are familiar today . . . and served them with a rich sauce and grated Parmesan cheese in a large china bowl. The first mouthful caused the illustrious epicure to shout, *"Cari!"* or in idiomatic English, "The darlings!" With the second mouthful, he emphasized his statement, exclaiming, "Ma Cari!" — "Ah, but what darlings!" And as the flavor of the dish grew upon him, his enthusiasm rose to even greater heights, and he cried out with joyful emotion, "Ma Caroni!" — "Ah, but dearest darlings!" In paying this supreme tribute to his cook's discovery, the nobleman bestowed the name by which this admirable preparation is known today . . . Macaroni!

According to Webster, macaroni is a "pasta first made in Italy, composed chiefly of wheat flour dried in the form of long slender tubes, and used, when dried, as an article of food." How drab a description of such a delightful dish! Not content simply with "long slender tubes," the citizens of each Italian community had their favorite ways of preparing macaroni. Romans prepared theirs in strips. In Bologna, they preferred flat ribbons; in Sicily, they rolled the pasta on knitting needles to form dried spirals. In any shape or form, macaroni, together with its brothers, cannot be dismissed as a mere "article of food." Macaroni is a feast with Italians and Americans alike!

Some shapes or varieties produced in Italy are not found in the United States. However, there are over 150 macaroni products produced here and a number of pasta products imported from Italy to please the most passionate pasta lover! From the wire-thin *capellini d'angelo* ("angel hair") to the giant cannelloni, macaroni sizes can run the gamut from spaghettini, spaghetti, vermicelli, maccaroncini, tufoli, zita to other odd shapes, including butterflies, stars, even conch shells.

Even more important than the size and shape is the nature of the sauce that accompanies the macaroni or spaghetti. Contrary to popular belief, not all macaroni sauces include tomato. For example, there is the "white" clam sauce of Naples, anchovy-garlic sauce, and pesto ("green") sauce of Genoa (a mixture of various fresh herbs, mixed with generous amounts of olive oil and garlic). Others prefer their noodles sauceless, with butter and Parmesan cheese in the famed fettuccine.

There is no end to the wonders that Italian cooks can create with pasta. Some find their way into lasagne in casseroles, sauced and combined with meatballs, or stuffed with meat or vegetarian delights as in manicotti (muffs) or cannoli. One rule of thumb applies to cooking all pasta, however. Do not overcook it. In fact, cook pasta *al dente* (to the tooth.)

Not all Italians share the same enthusiasm for macaroni. For example, the people of northern Italy are particularly fond of rice — hence their famous *risottos*. In other parts of Italy, *polenta* — the thick cornmeal mush — is a staple, combined with tomato paste or ripe tomatoes. Occasionally, a little grated cheese, pork and garlic are used to add flavor. Polenta is even eaten hot as it comes off the stove, or allowed to cool, sliced and fried in olive oil.

Gnocchi

Serves 6

1 can (10¾ ounces) condensed
  chicken broth
¾ cup milk
⅛ teaspoon ground nutmeg

⅔ cup cream of wheat cereal
1 cup freshly grated Romano cheese
2 eggs, slightly beaten
4 tablespoons butter or margarine

1. Combine broth, milk and nutmeg in saucepan; bring to boil.
2. Gradually add cereal, stirring constantly.
3. Reduce heat and cook mixture over low heat 10 minutes, or until very thick. Stir often.
4. Add ½ cup cheese, eggs, and 1 tablespoon butter, stirring vigorously until well blended.
5. Spread in buttered 2-quart shallow 12 x 8 x 2-inch baking dish or spread ½-inch thick on buttered cookie sheet; chill 1 hour or more.
6. Cut into 2-inch circles, dipping cutter into cold water.
7. Arrange circles overlapping in buttered 10-inch pie plate.
8. Melt remaining butter and pour over gnocchi.
9. Sprinkle with remaining cheese.
10. Broil 4 inches from heat source, or until lightly browned.

NOTE: To preserve the delicate flavor of these tender little dumplings, they should be cooked soon after preparing. They can also be served with your favorite tomato sauce.

Polenta

Serves 10

1 can (10¾ ounces) condensed
  chicken broth
1¾ cups water

1 cup cornmeal
1 tablespoon butter or margarine
freshly grated Parmesan cheese

1. Boil broth and ¾ cup water in saucepan. Let simmer.
2. Blend remaining water into cornmeal until smooth.
3. Pour cornmeal mixture into simmering broth, stirring constantly.
4. Cover and cook over low heat 15 minutes (mixture will be very thick), stirring often.
5. Stir in butter.
6. Spoon into buttered bowl and let stand 10 minutes.
7. Unmold onto flat plate. Cut into thick slices.
8. Serve with additional melted butter and freshly grated Parmesan cheese.

NOTE: Fried polenta is easy to prepare: Follow steps 1-5 above. Spoon into buttered 9 x 5 x 3-inch loaf pan. Chill. Cut into slices. Brown slices in butter. Serve piping hot.

Cannelloni

Serves 6

1½ cups all-purpose flour
1½ teaspoons salt
5 eggs, slightly beaten
1 tablespoon corn oil
½ cup chopped onion
1 medium clove garlic, minced
½ teaspoon basil leaves, crushed
2 tablespoons butter or margarine

2 cups Italian plum tomatoes, canned
 or fresh (16 ounces)
1 can (11 ounces) condensed cheddar
 cheese soup
½ cup milk
½ cup freshly grated Parmesan cheese
1½ cups ricotta cheese
½ cup chopped hard salami
¼ cup chopped prosciutto or boiled ham

1. Combine flour and salt in mixing bowl.
2. Add 3 eggs and corn oil. Mix with fork to form a firm dough.
3. Knead dough on lightly floured board until smooth, about 5 minutes.
4. Cover and let sit 5 minutes.
5. Roll dough into 12 x 18-inch rectangle.
6. Cut dough into eighteen 4 x 3-inch rectangles.
7. Cover and let sit 1 hour.
8. Cook pasta rectangles, a few at a time, in several quarts of boiling salt water for 5 minutes, or until tender.
9. Rinse in cold water; drain on damp towel.
10. Meanwhile, start sauce by combining onion, garlic and basil and cooking in butter in skillet until tender.
11. Add tomatoes and bring to boil.
12. Reduce heat and simmer 30 minutes, stirring occasionally.
13. Pour 1 cup sauce into bottom of 3-quart 13 x 9 x 2-inch shallow baking pan.
14. Prepare filling by combining soup, milk and Parmesan cheese in bowl.
15. Pour ½ soup mixture into saucepan and add remaining ingredients.
16. Cook filling, stirring until thickened.
17. To assemble, spoon 2 tablespoons of filling on narrow end of each pasta piece; roll up.
18. Place seam-side down in baking dish and spoon remaining soup mixture and sauce over cannelloni.
19. Bake in preheated 350° F. oven 30 to 35 minutes, or until hot.
20. Serve with additional Parmesan cheese, if desired.

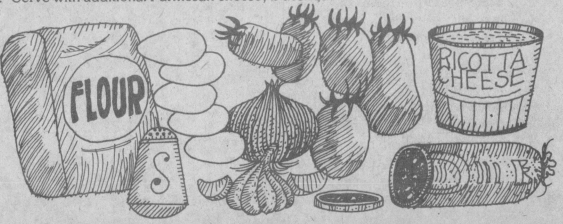

Clam Pantry Pasta

Serves 4 to 6

1 cup elbow or shell macaroni
1 cup green noodles
1½ quarts boiling water
1 teaspoon salt
2 cans (7½ ounces each)
   minced clams, undrained
1 tablespoon onion flakes

2 tablespoons butter or margarine
1 tablespoon flour
1/16 teaspoon instant garlic powder
1/16 teaspoon ground black pepper
⅓ cup milk
2 tablespoons parsley flakes
½ pint creamed cottage cheese

freshly grated Parmesan cheese

1. Cook macaroni and green noodles in boiling salted water 10 minutes.
2. Rinse, drain, and set aside.
3. Drain clams, reserving ¾ cup clam liquid; set clams aside.
4. Soften onion flakes in 2 tablespoons clam liquid; let stand 10 minutes.
5. Cook softened onion in hot butter over low heat until golden.
6. Remove from heat; stir in remaining clam liquid, flour, garlic powder, pepper and milk.
7. Return to low heat, stirring constantly until smooth and slightly thickened.
8. Stir in parsley flakes; set clam sauce mixture aside.
9. Layer half the cooked macaroni in shallow greased 1½-quart baking dish.
10. Spread evenly with cottage cheese and drained minced clams.
11. Cover clams with remaining pasta, pour clam sauce over all, and sprinkle top with Parmesan cheese.
12. Cover with foil and bake in preheated 350° F. oven 25 minutes, or until hot and bubbly.

Crab Manicotti

Serves 4 to 6

8 manicotti shells
1 package (6 ounces) frozen Alaska
   King crab, thawed and drained
   (reserve liquid)
1½ cups ricotta cheese
¼ cup chopped walnuts
2 tablespoons minced fresh
   parsley
1 tablespoon grated onion

1 can (15 ounces) tomato sauce
   with tomato bits
1 teaspoon sugar
½ cup chicken broth
½ teaspoon crushed basil
¼ teaspoon crushed oregano
¼ teaspoon crushed marjoram
⅛ teaspoon garlic powder
⅛ teaspoon whole thyme

1. Cook manicotti shells according to package directions.
2. Chop crab coarsely.
3. Add reserved crab liquid, ricotta, walnuts, parsley and onion; mix well.
4. Fill manicotti shells with crab mixture.
5. Place filled shells in well-buttered 11 x 7 x 1½-inch baking dish.
6. Combine remaining ingredients in medium-size saucepan.
7. Cook over medium heat 5 minutes, stirring often.
8. Pour over shells and bake in preheated 375° F. oven 30 minutes.

Homemade Fettuccine

Serves 6 to 8

2 cups all-purpose flour
1 large egg, plus 1 extra
  egg yolk

1 tablespoon fine-grade olive oil
scant teaspoon salt
¾ cup warm water

8 quarts salted boiling water

1. Put flour in large mixing bowl. Make a well in center.
2. Add eggs, oil and salt. Mix with wooden spoon until dough can be gathered into a ball.
3. Add a few drops of warm water, a drop at a time, mixing with spoon to form a ball.
4. Knead lightly on lightly floured board until smooth and elastic, about 10 minutes. (Add more flour if necessary.)
5. Wrap in waxed paper and let dough sit 10 minutes before rolling out.
6. Divide into halves. Cover one with waxed paper while you roll out the other half.
7. Flatten dough with floured hands. Roll out with rolling pin until paper thin.
8. Sprinkle very lightly with flour; let thin dough sit 10 minutes.
9. Repeat, using other half.
10. Carefully roll up dough jelly-roll fashion.
11. With very sharp knife, cut through rolls crosswise into ¼-inch strips.
12. Unroll strips; spread to dry on waxed paper.
13. When dry, cook in rapidly boiling salted water until al dente, about 5 to 7 minutes. (A little olive oil in the boiling water keeps noodles from sticking together.) Do not overcook.
14. Drain.

NOTE: Noodles need not be cooked at once. Cover tightly and store in plastic wrap in refrigerator up to 24 hours. Noodles can also be frozen.

Fettuccine Elegante

Serves 4

2 tablespoons butter
2 tablespoons chopped mild onions
1 clove fresh garlic, minced
1 cup fresh mushrooms, sliced
¼ pound thinly sliced ham

¼ cup white wine
1 cup heavy cream
1 cup freshly grated Parmesan cheese
½ pound cooked green fettuccine
4 sprigs parsley (for garnish)

1. Heat butter in skillet.
2. Add onions, garlic, mushrooms and ham; sauté until heated.
3. Add wine and heavy cream; bring to boil.
4. Add ⅔ cup Parmesan cheese and fettuccine, stirring constantly over medium heat until all ingredients are well mixed.
5. Reduce heat and keep warm for serving.
6. To serve, twirl four separate portions onto heated plates; sprinkle with remaining Parmesan cheese and garnish with parsley sprigs.

NOTE: Fine for an appetizer.

Fettuccine Carbonara

Serves 4 to 6

¼ pound bacon, diced
¼ cup chopped prosciutto
2 large cloves garlic, flattened
  but kept whole
1 teaspoon fine-grade olive oil
1 pound uncooked fettuccine noodles

3 eggs
½ cup freshly grated Romano
  cheese
freshly ground black pepper
  to taste
grated Parmesan cheese

1. Cook bacon just until crisp, but not browned.
2. Add prosciutto, garlic and oil to bacon; simmer.
3. Cook fettuccine in boiling salted water until al dente.
4. While fettuccine is cooking, beat eggs in a large bowl with ¼ cup Romano cheese.
5. Turn fettuccine into bowl with eggs and cheese; toss together quickly.
6. Remove garlic cloves from bacon mixture and toss mixture into eggs and fettuccine.
7. Serve piping hot, topped with pepper, remaining Romano cheese and Parmesan cheese.

NOTE: Speed and dexterity are the secret to the success of this classic Italian dish!

Green & Yellow Fettuccine
with Scallops & Zucchini

Serves 6

2 small zucchini
1 pound bay scallops
¾ cup butter
2 cloves garlic, minced
flour
2 tablespoons fresh basil or
  Italian parsley

½ teaspoon salt
freshly ground black pepper
1 pound fettuccine
½ pound green noodles
boiling salted water

1. Slice zucchini into lengthwise quarters, then into small pieces.
2. Cut scallops into small, even-size pieces; set aside.
3. Melt butter in large skillet.
4. When foam subsides, toss zucchini over medium flame for 2 to 3 minutes.
5. Add garlic.
6. Dredge scallops in flour; shake off excess flour.
7. Fry scallops quickly in skillet, moving zucchini to one side. Toss 1 to 2 minutes until lightly browned.
8. Add basil, salt and a few grains of black pepper.
9. Remove from heat.
10. Meanwhile, cook pasta in boiling salted water according to package directions until al dente.
11. Drain and toss immediately with scallop and zucchini butter.
12. Serve piping hot.

NOTE: Unusual and delicious!

Lasagna Verdi
(Spinach Lasagna)

Serves 6

½ cup minced onion
2 tablespoons butter or margarine
⅓ cup dry white wine
1 can (10½ ounces) condensed
   cream of chicken soup
2 packages (10 ounces each) frozen
   chopped spinach, cooked
   and well drained
1 cup grated Parmesan cheese

1 egg, slightly beaten
1 large clove garlic, minced
¼ teaspoon Italian seasoning, crushed
2 tablespoons olive oil
1 can (10¾ ounces) condensed
   tomato soup
½ cup water
12 lasagna noodles, cooked
   and drained

1. For filling, sauté onion in butter until tender.
2. Add wine; simmer a few minutes.
3. Blend in chicken soup, spinach, Parmesan cheese and egg.
4. Meanwhile, make sauce by cooking together garlic and Italian seasoning in olive oil.
5. Add soup and water; simmer 30 minutes.
6. Pour ½ sauce into greased 12 x 8 x 2-inch baking dish; top with 4 noodles.
7. Spread ½ of filling on top of noodles; top with 4 more noodles.
8. Spread remaining filling on noodles; top with remaining noodles and sauce.
9. Bake uncovered in preheated 350° F. oven 45 minutes, or until hot.
10. Let stand 15 minutes before serving (to firm up).

NOTE: Don't just think of lasagna as noodles with meat sauce and cheese! Italians are very inventive cooks, especially with these large flat noodles. This is a wonderful make-ahead dish, for flavor improves on the second day.

Macaroni with Broccoli, Calabrian Style

Serves 6

2 tablespoons 100% corn oil margarine
2 cloves garlic, minced
1 teaspoon oregano leaves
⅛ teaspoon ground black pepper
4 medium tomatoes, cut in wedges
   and halved
4 cups broccoli flowerets and
   stems

2 tablespoons chopped dark seedless
   raisins
2 tablespoons freshly grated Parmesan
   cheese
½ pound vermicelli or macaroni,
   prepared according to package
   directions and drained
2 tablespoons chopped fresh parsley

1. Heat margarine in Dutch oven over medium heat.
2. Add garlic, oregano and pepper; sauté until garlic is golden.
3. Mix in tomatoes and broccoli stems; simmer, uncovered, 5 minutes.
4. Add broccoli flowerets; cover and simmer 10 minutes.
5. Stir in raisins; cover and cook 3 minutes longer.
6. Toss prepared vegetable mixture and Parmesan cheese with drained hot vermicelli or macaroni.
7. Serve with parsley garnish.

Speedy Lasagna, Microwaved

Serves 6

½ pound lasagna
salt
3 quarts boiling water
½ pound lean ground beef

1 cup ricotta cheese
¼ pound mozzarella cheese, cubed
2 tablespoons grated Parmesan cheese
1 egg

1 cup prepared marinara sauce

1. Gradually add lasagna and 1 tablespoon salt to rapidly boiling water so that water continues to boil.
2. Cook, uncovered, stirring occasionally, for 5 minutes.
3. Drain in colander.
4. While the lasagna is cooking, place in food processor beef, cheese, egg, ⅔ cup marinara sauce and 1 teaspoon salt. Process until thoroughly mixed with cutting blade of food processor.
5. Arrange ⅓ of the lasagna in bottom of microwave-proof baking dish (about 10 x 6 x 2-inches).
6. Spread about half of meat mixture over it.
7. Repeat layers, ending with lasagna.
8. Spread remaining sauce over top.
9. Sprinkle with additional mozzarella and Parmesan cheese, if desired.
10. Cover and microwave 12 minutes, turning dish after 6 minutes.
11. Brown with browning unit or in broiler, if desired.

CONVENTIONAL METHOD: Grate mozzarella cheese. Mix together beef, cheeses, egg and ⅔ cup marinara sauce. Assemble as above. Bake, uncovered, in preheated 375° F. oven 20 minutes, or until bubbling.

Mushrooms Tagliarini

Serves 6

1 package (12 ounces) tagliarini
2 tablespoons sweet butter
½ cup olive oil
½ pound mushrooms, sliced
1 green pepper, diced

3 green onions, chopped
1 teaspoon sweet basil, crushed
½ teaspoon oregano, crushed
½ teaspoon salt
freshly grated Parmesan cheese

1. Cook tagliarini in boiling salted water until al dente.
2. Drain and run under cold water.
3. Meanwhile, combine butter and oil in skillet.
4. Sauté mushrooms, pepper and onions until tender.
5. Add basil, oregano and salt.
6. Add drained tagliarini and heat 2 to 3 minutes.
7. Sprinkle with Parmesan cheese and serve.

Linguini with Parsley Pesto Sauce

Serves 8

1 pound linguini or spaghetti
salt
4 to 6 quarts boiling water
1 cup parsley sprigs
½ cup pine nuts
2 cloves fresh garlic

1 tablespoon dried basil
½ cup olive oil
¼ cup water
½ cup freshly grated Parmesan
  cheese
dash pepper

1. Gradually add linguini and 2 tablespoons salt to rapidly boiling water so water continues to boil.
2. Cook, uncovered, stirring occasionally, until tender.
3. Drain in colander.
4. While linguini is cooking, combine in electric blender container parsley, nuts, garlic, basil, oil and water. Blend until smooth.
5. Gradually add cheese until well mixed.
6. Season to taste with salt and pepper.
7. Toss linguini with sauce and serve immediately.

CONVENTIONAL METHOD: Finely chop parsley and nuts; crush garlic. Thoroughly mix together with remaining ingredients in serving bowl.

Linguini con Cozze

Serves 4

24 mussels
water
¾ cup olive oil
2 cloves garlic, minced
½ dried chili pepper

2 tablespoons chopped fresh parsley
salt
½ cup dry white wine
1 pound linguini
freshly ground black pepper

freshly grated Parmesan or Romano cheese (optional)

1. Scrub mussels.
2. Cook in 2 quarts of water, shaking them over medium-high heat until shells open.
3. Discard unopened mussels; remove opened ones from their shells. Discard shells.
4. Heat oil in large skillet. Sauté garlic and chili pepper until garlic is golden. Cool.
5. Add mussels, 1 tablespoon parsley and salt to taste. Cook gently 5 minutes.
6. Add wine; cover and simmer 5 minutes.
7. Cook linguini in 6 quarts boiling water salted with 2 teaspoons salt. Cook until pasta is al dente.
8. Do **not** drain thoroughly; just remove pasta with a fork to large heated mixing bowl.
9. Add half the mussel mixture and toss well.
10. Top with remaining mussel mixture; sprinkle with remaining parsley.
11. Spoon into serving bowls. Season with freshly ground pepper to taste.
12. If desired, serve with freshly grated Parmesan or Romano cheese.

NOTE: Inexpensive and delicious!

Meatless Lasagna

Serves 8 to 10

¾ pound lasagna noodles
    (about 14 noodles)
2 tablespoons corn oil
1 medium onion, minced (1 cup)
2 cloves garlic, minced
1 can (29 ounces) tomato sauce
1 can (14½ ounces) whole tomatoes
1 can (6 ounces) tomato paste
2 teaspoons salt

1 teaspoon dried oregano leaves
½ teaspoon dried basil leaves
¼ teaspoon ground black pepper
1 teaspoon sugar
1 pint part-skim ricotta cheese
¼ cup skim milk
¼ cup freshly grated Parmesan
    cheese
2 tablespoons chopped fresh parsley

1 package (8 ounces) part-skim mozzarella cheese, sliced

1. Cook, rinse, and hold noodles according to package directions.
2. Heat corn oil in 5-quart saucepot over medium heat.
3. Add onion and garlic; sauté until tender.
4. Add tomato sauce, tomatoes, tomato paste, salt, oregano, basil, pepper and sugar.
5. Bring sauce to a boil; reduce heat, cover, and simmer for 1 hour, stirring often.
6. Meanwhile, stir together ricotta cheese, milk, 2 tablespoons Parmesan cheese and parsley in medium-size bowl.
7. Spoon 1 cup sauce into bottom of 13 x 9 x 2-inch baking pan.
8. Cover with 1 layer of noodles.
9. Spread with half of ricotta cheese mixture and top with half of mozzarella cheese slices.
10. Cover with sauce.
11. Repeat layering until all ingredients are used, ending with sauce.
12. Sprinkle top with remaining Parmesan cheese.
13. Bake in preheated 350° F. oven 30 to 45 minutes, or until bubbly and heated through.
14. Let sit 15 to 30 minutes before serving. Cut into squares.

Pasta in Vegetable Tomato Sauce

Serves 4 to 6

3 tablespoons olive oil
½ pound broccoli, chopped
    (about 2½ cups)
½ pound fresh mushrooms,
    chopped
1 cup finely chopped onion

2 cloves garlic, minced
2 cups fresh tomato sauce
    (see page 38)
1 pound green spinach
    noodles, cooked
grated Parmesan cheese

1. Heat oil in medium saucepan.
2. Add broccoli, mushrooms, onion and garlic; cook until tender.
3. Stir in tomato sauce. Bring to a boil.
4. Pour over hot, cooked pasta. Sprinkle with Parmesan cheese.

Baked Manicotti

Serves 6

2 cans (12 ounces each) low sodium
tomato juice
1 teaspoon oregano leaves
1 teaspoon basil leaves
½ teaspoon fresh garlic, crushed
¼ cup unsalted margarine
½ cup chopped onion
4 cups chopped fresh spinach
1 container (15 ounces) part-skim
ricotta cheese

¼ cup unsifted flour
⅛ teaspoon ground white pepper
⅛ teaspoon ground nutmeg
1 cup skim milk
12 manicotti shells, cooked
according to package directions
(without added salt) and drained
parsley (for garnish)

1. Combine tomato juice, oregano, basil and garlic in saucepan; bring to a boil.
2. Reduce heat to low and simmer until thickened and reduced to 2 cups.
3. Melt 1 tablespoon margarine in large skillet over medium heat.
4. Add onion and sauté until tender, 2 to 3 minutes.
5. Add spinach; toss and stir until wilted, about 2 minutes.
6. Remove skillet from heat and stir in ricotta cheese. Set aside.
7. Melt remaining margarine in a medium saucepan over low heat.
8. Stir in flour, pepper and nutmeg; gradually mix in milk.
9. Bring to a boil, stirring constantly. Cook and stir 1 minute, until thickened.
10. Stir half of prepared white sauce into spinach mixture.
11. Spoon mixture into manicotti shells.
12. Pour prepared tomato sauce into a 13 x 9 x 2-inch baking dish to completely cover the bottom.
13. Arrange stuffed manicotti in sauce.
14. Spoon remaining sauce over manicotti; top with spoonfuls of remaining white sauce.
15. Bake in preheated 375° F. oven 20 to 25 minutes, or until hot and bubbly.
16. Serve garnished with parsley.

Spaghetti with Anchovy Sauce

Serves 3 to 4

½ pound thin spaghetti
½ cup corn oil
¼ cup corn oil margarine

2 cloves garlic, sliced
1 can (2 ounces) anchovy fillets
3 tablespoons minced fresh parsley

1. Cook spaghetti according to package directions, omitting salt. Drain.
2. Meanwhile, 5 minutes before spaghetti is done, heat corn oil and margarine together in medium-size skillet over medium heat.
3. Add garlic and anchovies. Cook, stirring to mash anchovies, about 5 minutes, or until fillets disintegrate.
4. Remove from heat. Add parsley.
5. Toss with spaghetti until evenly coated.

Pollo alla Dante
(Manicotti)

Serves 4

For the Wine Sauce

½ cup butter or margarine
½ cup flour
1½ teaspoons salt
½ cup white wine

dash white pepper
1 cup milk
3½ cups chicken broth

1. Melt butter in heavy saucepan.
2. Blend in flour, salt, pepper, milk and 1 cup chicken broth.
3. Cook over medium heat, stirring frequently with wire whisk, until sauce thickens.
4. Pour off and reserve ⅓ cup sauce for filling.
5. Add 2½ cups chicken broth and wine to remaining sauce; bring to boil.

Filling

1½ cups cooked chicken
  or turkey, finely chopped
5 ounces Gruyere or Swiss cheese,
  grated
⅓ cup Wine Sauce
¼ cup white wine

1 egg, beaten
1 tablespoon minced parsley
1 clove garlic, crushed
1 package (3¾ ounces) manicotti
3 tablespoons freshly grated Parmesan
  cheese

1. Combine chicken, Gruyere cheese, Wine Sauce, wine, egg, parsley and garlic. Fill uncooked manicotti.
2. Cover bottom of 2-quart oblong baking dish with a little sauce.
3. Arrange manicotti in single layer, at least 1 inch apart. Add remaining sauce.
4. Cover and bake in preheated 350° F. oven 10 to 15 minutes.
5. Uncover, spoon unabsorbed sauce over manicotti, and sprinkle with Parmesan cheese.
6. Bake 10 to 15 minutes longer on top rack of oven or broil (if dish is broiler-proof) to brown lightly.

NOTE: A classic Italian dish.

Mostaccioli with Pepper & Tomatoes

Serves 4 to 6

1 green pepper	2 tablespoons Italian
1 red pepper	seasoning
1 cup plus 2 teaspoons	dash of crushed red pepper
olive oil	1 pound mostaccioli
15 cherry tomatoes, halved	3 tablespoons butter

1 cup freshly grated Parmesan cheese (more, if desired)

1. Rub peppers with 1 teaspoon olive oil.
2. Place in shallow baking dish and roast in preheated 400° F. oven a few minutes, or until peppers are brown and skin is wrinkled.
3. Cool. Remove skin and slice peppers into 1-inch strips.
4. Place pepper strips in large mixing bowl; add cherry tomatoes, remaining olive oil, Italian seasoning and crushed red pepper. Mix, cover, and marinate at room temperature 8 hours.
5. Cook mostaccioli in boiling salted water until al dente.
6. Drain, rinse with cold water and set aside.
7. Heat butter in large pot over medium heat. Add mostaccioli and cook to coat with butter.
8. Add pepper-tomato mixture. Continue cooking until sauce and pasta are hot.
9. Remove from heat and transfer to large serving bowl. Toss with Parmesan cheese and serve at once.

Zucchini Mescolanza
(Mixed-Up Zucchini)

Serves 6

½ pound ground lean beef	1 can (2¼ ounces) ripe olives,
1 cup chopped onion	drained and sliced
1 clove garlic, minced	1 teaspoon salt
3 cups sliced zucchini	¼ teaspoon freshly ground
2 cans (15 ounces each)	black pepper
marinara sauce	1 package (14 ounces) mostaccioli

freshly grated Parmesan cheese (for garnish)

1. Cook beef, onion and garlic until light brown.
2. Add zucchini, marinara sauce, olives, salt and pepper; simmer 10 minutes, or until zucchini is tender.
3. Cook mostaccioli as directed on package.
4. Serve mostaccioli with zucchini sauce; garnish with Parmesan cheese.

NOTE: In Italian, mescolanza means a "mixed-up creation"!

Noodles Alfredo

Serves 2

4 ounces medium egg noodles
  (about 2½ cups)
1½ teaspoons salt
1½ quarts boiling water

2 tablespoons butter or margarine
⅓ cup half-and-half
⅓ cup freshly grated Parmesan
  cheese

1. Gradually add noodles and salt to rapidly boiling water so that water continues to boil.
2. Cook, uncovered, stirring occasionally, until tender.
3. Drain in colander.
4. Put butter and half-and-half in same pot. Heat slowly until butter melts.
5. Add noodles and cheese. Toss gently until noodles are well coated.
6. Cook and stir over low heat until noodles are hot.
7. Serve half immediately; freeze remainder for another meal.

MICROWAVE REHEATING: Cover frozen microwave-proof casserole in microwave about 6 minutes, or until hot.

CONVENTIONAL REHEATING: Cover frozen casserole and bake in preheated 375° F. oven 35 minutes, or until hot.

Stuffed Pasta Shells

Serves 4

2 cans (6½ ounces each) chunk
  light tuna
1 container (16 ounces) ricotta
  cheese
½ cup chopped green onion
⅓ cup grated Parmesan cheese
⅓ cup toasted slivered almonds
16 jumbo pasta shells
1 large onion, chopped

1 clove garlic, minced
1 tablespoon olive oil
1 can (14½ ounces) Italian-
  style tomatoes
1 can (8 ounces) tomato sauce
¼ cup dry red wine
1 teaspoon sweet basil
1 teaspoon salt
¼ teaspoon oregano

1. Drain and flake tuna.
2. Combine tuna with ricotta cheese, onion, Parmesan cheese and almonds.
3. Cook pasta shells according to package directions.
4. Fill cooked shells with tuna mixture.
5. Sauté onion and garlic in oil; stir in undrained tomatoes, tomato sauce, wine, basil, salt and oregano. Simmer 20 minutes.
6. Spoon one-fourth of sauce mixture into shallow 2-quart casserole; arrange stuffed shells over sauce.
7. Pour remaining sauce over shells. Cover with foil and bake in preheated 350° F. oven 15 minutes.
8. Remove foil and bake 15 minutes longer.

Pasta Primavera

Serves 4 to 6

⅓ cup corn oil
¼ pound mushrooms, sliced (1½ cups)
1 medium onion, cut into very thin wedges (about ½ cup)
2 cloves garlic, minced or pressed
½ pound broccoli, cut into flowerets (2 cups)
1 medium zucchini, sliced and halved (2 cups)

2 carrots, cut into julienne strips (1 cup)
⅓ cup dry white wine
¼ cup chopped parsley
1 teaspoon dried basil leaves
½ teaspoon salt
⅛ teaspoon pepper
½ pound spaghetti, cooked
½ cup freshly grated Parmesan cheese

1. Heat corn oil in large skillet over medium-high heat.
2. Add mushrooms, onion and garlic; cook, stirring frequently 1 to 2 minutes.
3. Add broccoli, zucchini and carrots; cook, stirring frequently 2 to 3 minutes.
4. Stir in wine, parsley, basil, salt and pepper; simmer 4 to 5 minutes, or until vegetables are tender-crisp.
5. Cook spaghetti according to package directions.
6. Toss together hot, cooked spaghetti, vegetable sauce and cheese. Serve at once.

Spaghetti & Clam Sauce

Serves 8

2 cans (8 ounces each) minced clams
½ cup salad oil
1 cup sweet onion, finely chopped
2 large fresh garlic cloves, minced
6 tablespoons butter or margarine
¾ cup dry white wine

¾ cup chicken broth or bouillon
½ teaspoon oregano, crushed
¾ cup freshly grated Parmesan or Romano cheese
pepper to taste
1 pound spaghetti
2 tablespoons salt
4 to 6 quarts boiling water

1. Drain juice from clams, reserving ½ cup juice. Set juice and clams aside.
2. Heat oil in large skillet. Add onion and garlic; sauté until tender, about 3 to 5 minutes.
3. Stir in butter, wine, chicken broth, oregano and reserved clam juice; simmer sauce, uncovered, 20 minutes.
4. Add drained clams to sauce and heat gently.
5. Remove from heat and stir in ¼ cup grated cheese and pepper.
6. Meanwhile, gradually add spaghetti and salt to rapidly boiling water so that water continues to boil. Cook, uncovered, stirring occasionally until tender.
7. Drain in colander.
8. Serve spaghetti with sauce and remaining grated cheese.

Spaghetti & Cod Fish, Italian Style

Serves 4 to 6

1 pound dry salt cod fish
2 medium onions, sliced
¼ cup olive or corn oil
1 can (16 ounces) tomatoes
¼ teaspoon ground black pepper

⅛ teaspoon cayenne
1 teaspoon Angostura
  aromatic bitters
salt to taste
1 pound spaghetti

1. A day ahead, cut dried cod fish into 3-inch squares.
2. Soak in cold water to cover for at least 18 hours, changing water three or four times.
3. On day of serving, sauté onions in oil until soft but not brown.
4. Add tomatoes, pepper and cayenne; simmer gently over low heat 45 minutes.
5. Add soaked, drained fish and Angostura aromatic bitters. Cover and cook over low heat about 45 minutes, or until fish is tender and flakes easily.
6. Taste to correct seasonings.
7. Cook spaghetti according to package directions.
8. Pour cod sauce over spaghetti and serve.

Spaghetti with Spinach Sauce

Serves 6

2 tablespoons salt
4 to 6 quarts boiling water
1 pound spaghetti
1 cup firmly packed spinach
  leaves
¼ cup firmly packed parsley
  leaves
1 small clove garlic
¼ cup butter or margarine

¼ cup olive oil
¼ cup pine nuts
2 tablespoons chopped walnuts
¼ cup freshly grated
  Romano cheese
¼ cup freshly grated
  Parmesan cheese
¾ teaspoon salt
½ teaspoon dried basil

1. Add 2 tablespoons salt to rapidly boiling water.
2. Gradually add spaghetti so water continues to boil.
3. Cook, uncovered, stirring occassionally, until tender.
4. Drain in colander.
5. Wash spinach and parsley; shake to remove excess water, but allow moisture to cling to leaves.
6. Place remaining ingredients in electric blender; blend at high speed until mixture looks like a thick purée, but with some specks of spinach and parsley still visible. (If sauce seems to thick, add a small amount of water.)
7. Pour mixture over spaghetti and toss until completely coated.

31

Spaghetti with Vegetable Sauce

Serves 8

1 pound spaghetti
salt
4 to 6 quarts boiling water
½ cup parsley sprigs
½ pound green beans, cut in thirds
1 pound tomatoes, cut in wedges
1 jar (16 ounces) onions, drained
1 clove fresh garlic, peeled

½ teaspoon chili powder
⅛ teaspoon pepper
1 can (10¾ ounces) condensed
  tomato soup
⅔ cup water
1 pound yellow squash
½ cup freshly grated Parmesan
  or Romano cheese

1. Gradually add spaghetti and 2 tablespoons salt to rapidly boiling water so that water continues to boil.
2. Cook, uncovered, stirring occasionally, until tender.
3. Drain in colander.
4. While spaghetti is cooking, process parsley in food processor; remove half the parsley and set aside.
5. Add to parsley in processor beans and half the tomatoes; process until tomatoes are puréed.
6. Add remaining tomatoes, onions, garlic, chili powder, pepper and ½ teaspoon salt; process until finely chopped.
7. Combine processed vegetable mixture, soup and ⅔ cup water in large microwave-proof bowl.
8. Slice squash with slicing disc in food processor; add to bowl.
9. Cover and microwave 12 minutes, stirring after 6 minutes.
10. Stir in cheese.
11. Pour sauce over hot spaghetti and garnish with reserved parsley.

CONVENTIONAL METHOD: Finely chop parsley and garlic. Coarsely chop tomatoes and onions. Thinly slice green beans and squash. Combine all ingredients except cheese in large saucepan. Heat to boiling, stirring occasionally. Simmer 5 minutes. Stir in cheese and serve over spaghetti.

Vermicelli Italiano

Serves 6

1 pound long vermicelli
¾ cup olive oil
2 cloves garlic, crushed
2 tablespoons chopped parsley
½ teaspoon Italian herbs

⅛ teaspoon freshly ground
  black pepper
¼ teaspoon salt
½ cup freshly grated
  Parmesan cheese

1. Cook vermicelli as directed on package.
2. Heat garlic in olive oil; stir in parsley, herbs, pepper and salt.
3. Add cooked vermicelli. Toss with Parmesan cheese.

NOTE: Authentically Italian!

Italian-Style Spaghetti with Scallop Sauce

Serves 4 to 6

1 pound scallops, preferably fresh
¼ pound butter
½ cup chopped onion
2 cloves garlic, chopped
¼ cup minced parsley
2 cans (8 ounces each) tomato sauce
   with mushrooms

¼ teaspoon paprika
½ teaspoon salt
dash freshly ground black pepper
1 pound spaghetti, cooked and
   drained
freshly grated Parmesan or
   Romano cheese

1. Cut large scallops in halves.
2. Heat butter in large saucepan.
3. Add onion, garlic and parsley; cook until onion is tender.
4. Add tomato sauce, paprika, salt, pepper and scallops; simmer 20 minutes, stirring often.
5. Serve over hot spaghetti. Sprinkle with grated cheese.

Stuffed Manicotti with Sherry Sauce

Serves 6

2 cans (6½ ounces each)
   chunk light tuna
1 package (10 ounces) frozen
   chopped spinach
1 package (8 ounces) ricotta cheese
1 egg, lightly beaten

1½ teaspoons salt
¼ teaspoon nutmeg
12 manicotti shells
2 quarts boiling water
Sherry Sauce
¼ cup grated Parmesan cheese

1. Drain tuna; set aside.
2. Cook spinach according to package directions.
3. Drain thoroughly in a sieve, pressing out excess water.
4. Combine spinach, ricotta, egg, seasonings and tuna; set aside.
5. Cook manicotti shells in boiling water 8 to 10 minutes until tender but still firm.
6. Drain.
7. Fill with tuna mixture.
8. Arrange in a well-buttered 2-quart baking dish.
9. Pour Sherry Sauce over all; sprinkle with Parmesan cheese.
10. Bake in preheated 350° F. oven for 30 minutes.

Sherry Sauce

2 tablespoons butter
2½ tablespoons flour

½ teaspoon salt
2 cups milk

2 tablespoons pale dry sherry

1. Melt butter; stir in flour and salt until blended.
2. Gradually add in milk, stirring constantly until mixture boils and thickens.
3. Remove from heat; stir in sherry.

Fenella Pearson's Tagliatelle Verdi al Gorgonzola
(Green Noodles with Gorgonzola Sauce)

Serves 6

4 tablespoons butter
2 ounces Gorgonzola cheese,
   crumbled (or other hard
   blue cheese)
about ½ cup heavy cream

1 pound green (spinach) noodles
boiling salted water
salt to taste
freshly ground pepper
   to taste

1. Melt butter in saucepan over low heat.
2. Add crumbled cheese, stirring until melted and smooth.
3. Stir in cream, adding enough to make sauce thickened but fluid.
4. Meanwhile, add noodles, little by little, to boiling salted water. Test frequently to be sure to avoid overcooking. Cook until al dente.
5. Remove noodles from heat; add 1 cup of cold water to stop boiling and drain at once.
6. Place in serving dish; pour sauce over it, toss to blend, and season as needed. Serve at once.

NOTE: Do **not** serve with Parmesan cheese! The secret to this dish is timing – getting noodles and sauce ready at the same time!

Tagliarini-Salami Toss

Serves 4

1 small onion, chopped
¼ cup butter
½ cup dry salami, cut in
   julienne strips
2 ounces cooked ham, cut in
   julienne strips
1 package (10 ounces) tagliarini or
   other fresh egg noodles

2 egg yolks, beaten
⅓ cup chopped fresh parsley
1 green onion, chopped
¾ cup diced Gruyere cheese
1 cup freshly grated Parmesan
   cheese
freshly ground black pepper
   to taste

1. Sauté onion in 1 tablespoon butter until softened.
2. Add salami and ham; heat through.
3. Melt remaining butter and set aside.
4. Cook pasta in boiling salted water as directed on package until barely al dente.
5. Drain and place in heated bowl.
6. Pour over pasta melted butter, egg yolks, salami-ham mixture, parsley, green onion, Gruyere cheese and half of Parmesan cheese.
7. Toss lightly, coating noodles well.
8. Grind pepper over all and serve. (Pass remaining Parmesan at the table.)

Mushroom Zucchini Risotto

Serves 6

¼ cup butter
2½ cups sliced fresh mushrooms
2½ cups sliced zucchini
2 tablespoons minced onion
½ teaspoon minced fresh garlic

1 cup uncooked Italian or converted rice
1 cup dry Marsala wine
2 cups broth (beef, chicken or vegetable)
salt to taste
pepper to taste

1. Melt 2 tablespoons butter in a large skillet over medium heat.
2. Add mushrooms, zucchini, onion and garlic; sauté until tender-crisp, about 5 minutes, stirring constantly.
3. Remove from pan and set aside.
4. Melt remaining 2 tablespoons butter in same skillet over medium heat.
5. Add rice and sauté 1 minute.
6. Stir in wine; cook over medium-high heat, stirring occasionally, until wine is absorbed.
7. Add ½ cup broth; cook, stirring occasionally, until broth is absorbed.
8. Continue adding broth and cooking until rice is al dente, about 15 minutes.
9. Toss in reserved vegetable mixture; cook 1 minute.
10. Season to taste with salt and pepper. Serve hot.

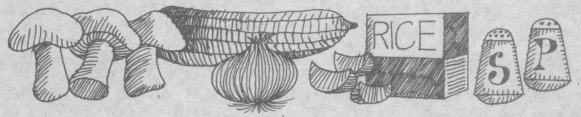

Risotto Portofino

Serves 6

1 cup chopped onion
1 clove garlic, crushed
3 tablespoons butter or
  margarine
1 cup uncooked rice
2 medium tomatoes, cut
  into eighths
1½ cups chicken broth

1 teaspoon salt
¼ teaspoon freshly ground
  black pepper
¼ teaspoon rosemary,
  crushed
1 bay leaf
1 can (4 ounces) sliced mushrooms,
  drained

1 pound shrimp, peeled, deveined and chopped

1. Cook onions and garlic in butter until onions are tender but not brown.
2. Add rice and cook 2 minutes longer.
3. Add remaining ingredients except shrimp.
4. Heat to boiling; stir once.
5. Cover, reduce heat, and simmer 20 minutes.
6. Add shrimp, cover, and cook 2 minutes longer. (If rice is too moist, allow to stand, covered, 10 minutes.)
7. Remove bay leaf and serve.

Rice Italianate

Serves 6

4 cups hot cooked rice
2 tablespoons butter or
  margarine, melted

⅓ cup grated Parmesan cheese
⅓ cup grated Swiss cheese
½ cup hot heavy cream
coarsely ground black pepper

1. Combine rice with butter and cheese. Mix with a fork, making certain rice kernels are well coated.
2. Pour cream over all and mix lightly.
3. Sprinkle with pepper and serve at once.

Risotto

Serves 6

1 cup uncooked rice
2 tablespoons butter,
  margarine or oil
½ cup chopped onions

½ cup diced green pepper
2 cups chicken broth
1 teaspoon salt
1 can (4 ounces) mushrooms, drained
½ cup freshly grated Parmesan cheese

1. Cook rice in butter until golden.
2. Add onions and green pepper; continue cooking 2 to 3 minutes, stirring constantly to prevent over-browning.
3. Add chicken broth, salt and mushrooms. Heat to boiling; stir.
4. Reduce heat, cover, and simmer 15 minutes, or until rice is tender and liquid is absorbed.
5. Remove from heat. Toss lightly with Parmesan cheese.

Savory Risotto

Serves 6

4 tablespoons butter
  or margarine
1 medium onion, chopped
½ cup sliced celery
¼ cup chopped green pepper

1 cup converted rice
½ cup Verdicchio white wine
1 can (13¾ ounces) chicken broth
½ teaspoon salt
dash thyme

1. Melt butter in large saucepan.
2. Sauté onion, celery and pepper in melted butter 5 minutes.
3. Add rice; continue cooking and stirring until rice becomes transparent.
4. Stir in wine, chicken broth, salt and thyme; bring to a boil.
5. Pour into greased 1½-quart casserole. Bake in preheated 350° F. oven 30 minutes.

Garlic Oil Sauce

Makes ⅔ cup

3 cloves fresh garlic,
  peeled and crushed

⅔ cup top-grade olive oil
  fresh or dried sweet basil

1 teaspoon salt

1. Heat garlic and oil together in small skillet.
2. Add basil and salt to taste.
3. Press garlic with a wooden spoon as it cooks to impart flavor to oil.

NOTE: Great spooned over hot cooked spaghetti, sprinkled with freshly grated black pepper and a generous amount of freshly grated Parmesan cheese!

Pasta con Pesto

Makes 1½ cups

For the Pesto

2 cups packed fresh basil leaves,
  washed and well drained
1 cup grated Romano cheese,
  plus additional cheese, if desired

½ cup olive oil
½ cup melted butter
6 large cloves fresh garlic,
  crushed

1. Place basil, cheese, oil and butter and garlic in a blender.
2. Begin blending, turning motor on and off.
3. Push pesto down from sides of blender with rubber spatula and continue blending until you have a very coarse purée.

For the Pasta

Serves 4 to 6

1 pound spaghetti, flat noodles or similar pasta, cooked
according to package directions and drained well
½ cup grated Romano cheese

1. Spoon 1 cup Pesto Sauce over hot, freshly cooked spaghetti; mix quickly with two forks.
2. Add ½ cup cheese and mix.
3. Serve with additional Pesto Sauce and cheese if desired.
4. Cover and refrigerate any leftover pesto up to a week, or freeze in small portions. (Surface will darken when exposed to air, so stir pesto before serving.)

Calamari Sauce for Pasta

Makes enough sauce for 4

1½ pounds fresh squid
3 tablespoons fine-grade olive oil
3 tablespoons sweet butter
4 tablespoons chopped salt pork
   (optional)
1 medium onion, chopped
2 cloves fresh garlic, peeled
12 sprigs fresh Italian parsley,
   leaves only
pinch red pepper

1 teaspoon freshly ground black pepper
½ cup dry red Italian wine
3 tablespoons freshly grated Romano cheese
1 can (16 ounces) peeled plum tomatoes,
   finely chopped
1 can (6 ounces) tomato paste
½ teaspoon salt
1½ teaspoons dried oregano leaves,
   crumbled
1 teaspoon marjoram leaves, crumbled

6 anchovy fillets, mashed (optional)

1. Wash and clean squid or buy cleaned squid from fish market. Pat-dry and dice.
2. Combine olive oil, butter and salt pork in skillet; heat.
3. Add onion and cook over medium heat, stirring until golden.
4. Add squid; stir and cook slowly 15 to 20 minutes.
5. Chop garlic and parsley together; add to squid mixture with red and black pepper.
6. Cook and stir 2 minutes over low heat.
7. Add wine; cover and simmer 5 minutes.
8. Add remaining ingredients except anchovy fillets. Stir, cover, and cook slowly 1 hour, or until sauce is reduced in volume.
9. Taste to correct seasoning. (If too salty, add more water and cook to reduce in volume.)
10. If desired, add anchovy fillets just before serving over hot cooked pasta.

Fresh Tomato Sauce

Makes 2 cups

6 medium fresh California tomatoes,
   peeled, cored and coarsely chopped
   (about 3 cups)
2 tablespoons olive oil
1 cup chopped onion
½ cup chopped green pepper
1 clove garlic, minced or pressed

2 tablespoons chopped fresh
   parsley
½ teaspoon salt
½ teaspoon basil leaves,
   crushed
¼ teaspoon oregano leaves,
   crushed

⅛ teaspoon pepper

1. In food processor or electric blender, purée 1½ cups chopped tomatoes; set aside.
2. Heat oil in large saucepan.
3. Add onion, green pepper and garlic; cook until tender.
4. Stir in chopped and puréed tomatoes, salt, basil, parsley, oregano and pepper. Cook over medium-low heat, stirring occasionally, until thickened, 40 to 45 minutes.
5. Cool. (Freeze, if desired.) Serve over fish, pasta, poultry or vegetables.

NOTE: A wonderful sauce to make with garden-ripe tomatoes and fresh herbs!

Spaghetti Meat Sauce I

Makes about 6½ quarts

½ cup corn oil
4 pounds ground beef
1½ quarts minced onion
   (about 12 medium)
3 cups chopped green pepper
   (about 4 large)
8 cloves garlic, minced
6 cans (1 pound each) tomatoes
1 can (29 ounces) tomato purée

4 cans (6 ounces each) tomato paste
½ cup chopped fresh parsley
¼ cup salt
2 tablespoons sugar
1 tablespoon freshly ground black
   pepper
3 bay leaves
1 tablespoon dried oregano leaves
1 teaspoon dried basil leaves

1. Heat corn oil in large (10-quart) heavy saucepot over medium heat.
2. Add beef, onion, green pepper and garlic; cook, stirring frequently, 20 to 30 minutes, or until meat is no longer red and fat has cooked out of meat. Skim off fat.
3. Add tomatoes, tomato purée, tomato paste, parsley, salt, sugar, pepper, bay leaves, oregano and basil. Cook, uncovered, over low heat, 1½ to 2 hours, stirring occasionally to break up tomatoes and skimming off fat as needed.
4. Remove bay leaves and serve over hot cooked spaghetti.

NOTE: To freeze sauce: Cool hot sauce quickly by placing saucepot in pan of ice or very cold water, stirring sauce frequently and changing water and adding ice as needed. Pour cooked sauce in serving portions into plastic or glass freezer containers, leaving ½-inch headspace to allow sauce to expand when frozen. Seal, label, and freeze. Sauce may be held up to 9 months. Thaw in refrigerator or turn into saucepan and reheat over very low heat, stirring frequently.

Spaghetti Meat Sauce II

Serves 10

1 large onion
2 medium-size carrots
1 small stalk celery
2 cloves garlic
1 teaspoon chopped parsley
1 tablespoon olive oil
2 pounds lean ground beef
¼ teaspoon salt

¼ teaspoon freshly ground
   black pepper
⅛ teaspoon ground cloves
⅛ teaspoon ground cinnamon
⅛ teaspoon ground nutmeg
⅛ teaspoon ground allspice
4 cans (6 ounces each) or ¾ pound
   sun-dried tomato paste (page 40)

water to dilute paste to consistency of light cream

1. Chop together onion, carrots, celery, garlic and parsley.
2. Brown in olive oil, then add beef.
3. Brown.
4. Season with salt, pepper, and spices.
5. Add diluted tomato paste and cook until well blended and meat is well done.
6. Serve over hot cooked spaghetti, sprinkled with grated cheese.

NOTE: Use 1 pound spaghetti with this amount of sauce.

Sun-Dried Italian Tomato Paste

4 quarts ripe tomatoes, sliced
2 tablespoons finely chopped
  basil leaves
2 teaspoons salt
½ cup chopped celery

2 carrots, scraped and sliced
1 large white onion, sliced
1-inch piece stick cinnamon
½ teaspoon peppercorns
½ teaspoon cloves

1. Combine all ingredients and simmer until very soft.
2. Put through sieve or food mill.
3. Cook in double boiler or heavy pan set on asbestos mat until very thick (about 3 hours).
4. Spread ½-inch thick on platters set in cold water to cool.
5. Cover with net or screen and dry in sun (6 to 8 hours) or in slow oven 250° F.
6. Pack in pieces in tin box with waxed paper between layers. Use in small amounts to season soups and to give added character to sauces.

NOTE: This is a recipe handed down in an old Italian family. It gives extraordinary flavor to food!

Ragu Bolognese
(Bolognese Meat Sauce)

Makes 1½ quarts

¾ cup onion flakes
¼ cup celery flakes
1⅓ cups water
2 tablespoons butter or
  margarine
½ cup coarsely chopped
  smoked ham
⅓ cup minced carrots
2 tablespoons olive oil
1 pound lean ground beef
½ cup dry white wine

1 can (10½ ounces) condensed
  beef broth
2 tablespoons tomato paste
1 tablespoon basil leaves,
  crumbled
¼ teaspoon garlic powder
⅛ teaspoon salt
⅛ teaspoon ground black
  pepper
1/16 teaspoon ground nutmeg
1 cup heavy cream

1. Rehydrate onion and celery flakes in ⅔ cup water for 10 minutes.
2. Melt butter in large skillet.
3. Add onion and celery, ham and carrots; sauté 8 to 10 minutes, stirring constantly.
4. Turn into a heavy saucepan; set aside.
5. Heat oil in the same skillet. Add beef and brown, stirring.
6. Add wine and cook over high heat until liquid evaporates.
7. Add meat to saucepan along with broth, tomato paste and remaining water; mix well.
8. Simmer, covered, 35 minutes, stirring occasionally.
9. Add seasonings and cook 10 minutes longer.
10. Stir in cream; heat, do not boil. Serve over spaghetti.

Pesto Genovese
(Pesto Sauce for Pasta)

Makes about 1¼ cups

2 cups fresh basil leaves,
tightly packed
½ cup freshly grated Parmesan
or Pecorino cheese
⅓ cup pine nuts
⅓ cup parsley
½ cup olive oil
½ teaspoon salt
4 large cloves garlic, peeled

1. Put all ingredients in electric blender.
2. Cover and process until smooth and creamy.
3. Keeps well refrigerated, with a layer of olive oil over the top surface, or freeze if desired.

NOTE: If desired, pesto can be made in the old-fashioned way with a mortar and pestle.

Salsa di Pomodori
(Basic Tomato Sauce)

Makes 4 cups

1 pound hot Italian sausages,
cut in 3-inch pieces
½ cup minced onion
½ teaspoon oregano leaves,
crushed
1 large clove garlic, minced
1 tablespoon olive oil
1 can (10¾ ounces) condensed
tomato soup
1 soup can water
1 can (6 ounces) tomato paste
2 tablespoons grated Parmesan
cheese
1 small bay leaf

1. Cook sausage in saucepan; pour off fat.
2. Add onion, oregano, garlic and olive oil. Cook until onion is tender.
3. Blend in remaining ingredients. Bring to boil; reduce heat and simmer 30 minutes, stirring occasionally.
4. Remove bay leaf. Serve over spaghetti.

NOTE: This basic sauce is delicious on virtually every kind of pasta — from spaghettini, a very thin spaghetti, to lasagna. Makes enough sauce to cover ½ pound cooked pasta. Double the recipe and freeze half for future "frozen assets."

Salsa di Fegatini di Pollo
(Chicken Livers Sauce)

Serves 3 to 4

1 pound fresh mushrooms
1 can (1 pound) whole peeled
  tomatoes
¼ cup butter or margarine
¼ cup minced onion
1 clove garlic, pressed

½ pound chicken livers, quartered
¼ cup Marsala wine
1 tablespoon flour
1 teaspoon sage
¾ teaspoon salt
freshly ground black pepper

steamed rice pasta (optional)

1. Rinse, pat dry, and slice mushrooms (makes about 5 cups); set aside.
2. Drain tomatoes, reserving juice. Chop tomatoes and set aside.
3. Melt butter in large skillet. Add onion and garlic; sauté until onions are limp.
4. Add mushrooms and chicken livers; sauté until livers are browned.
5. Add wine, flour, sage, salt, black pepper and reserved tomatoes and juice. Simmer, uncovered, until hot, stirring occasionally, 10 minutes.
6. Serve over steamed rice pasta, if desired.

Peanut Butter Tomato Sauce

Makes 1 quart

2 tablespoons corn oil
½ cup coarsely chopped onion
½ cup coarsely chopped
  green pepper
1 small zucchini, diced
  (about 1 cup)
1 clove garlic, minced or pressed
1 can (16 ounces) tomatoes,
  chopped
1 can (8 ounces) tomato sauce

1 can (8¾ ounces) red kidney
  beans, drained
¼ cup super-chunk peanut butter
1 teaspoon dried oregano
  leaves
½ teaspoon salt
½ teaspoon dried basil leaves
⅛ teaspoon crushed dried red
  pepper
1 bay leaf

1. Heat corn oil in 5-quart Dutch oven over medium heat.
2. Add onion, green pepper, zucchini and garlic; cook 5 minutes or until tender, stirring occasionally.
3. Stir in tomatoes, tomato sauce, beans, peanut butter, oregano, salt, basil, red pepper and bay leaf. Cover and cook 30 minutes, or until flavors are blended, stirring occasionally.
4. Serve over hot cooked spaghetti.

NOTE: Makes enough sauce to cover 1 pound spaghetti. Sauce may be frozen and reheated gently over medium heat, stirring occasionally.

Carciofi Ripieni con Granchio
(Artichokes Stuffed with Crabmeat)

Serves 8

cold water
4 lemons
8 large artichokes
1 cup dry white wine
olive oil
2 red peppers, roasted and chopped
  (about ½ cup chopped)
1 pound crabmeat

1 small bottle capers, drained
2 tablespoons Dijon-style mustard
small bunch Italian parsley
dash Tabasco sauce
½ tablespoon brandy
freshly ground black pepper
salt
¼ cup bread crumbs

1. Prepare a large bowl of cold water diluted with juice from 1 lemon. Set aside.
2. Prepare artichokes as follows:
   a. Cut off stems from artichokes flush with bottoms.
   b. Pull off outer leaves of each artichoke, snapping each leaf backward to where it breaks off naturally, working around artichokes in spiral fashion.
   c. Continue this until only light-green inner leaves remain.
   d. Slice off all leaves so only artichoke bottoms remain.
   e. Use spoon to scrape out hairy choke, placing each artichoke as it is completed in bowl of lemon-water.
3. Heat 2 cups water in saucepan with wine and 2 to 3 tablespoons olive oil.
4. Add artichokes; cover and simmer 30 minutes, or until tender.
5. Prepare filling as follows:
   a. Roast peppers directly on high gas flame, turning so skin blackens evenly.
   b. Cool several minutes.
   c. Peel off skin; remove and discard seeds and inner membrane.
   d. Mince peppers and set aside.
6. Spread crabmeat on tray and pick through carefully to remove any bits of shell.
7. Place crabmeat and peppers in mixing bowl; add 2 tablespoons drained capers, mustard, ¼ cup chopped parsley, 2 to 3 drops Tabasco, ¼ cup olive oil, juice of remaining lemons, splash of brandy, pepper and salt to taste and enough bread crumbs to bind mixture without being too dry.
8. Divide filling among artichoke bottoms, mounding it with hands into dome shape.
9. Place stuffed artichokes in baking dish. Bake in preheated 375° F. oven 20 to 25 minutes, or until brown and crusty on top.
10. Serve with lemon wedges.

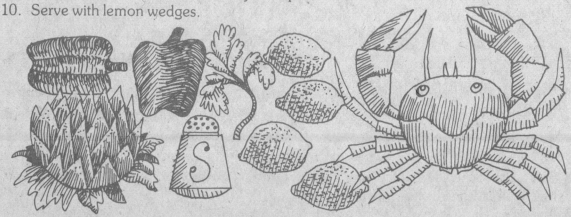

Eggplant Parmesan

Serves 6

1 stick 100% corn oil margarine
¼ cup chopped onion
2 cans (8 ounces each) tomato sauce
½ teaspoon oregano leaves, crushed
½ teaspoon salt

1 large (1½ pound) eggplant, peeled and cut in ½-inch slices
1 pound skimmed-milk mozzarella cheese, thinly sliced
3 teaspoons grated Parmesan cheese

1. Melt 1 tablespoon margarine in saucepan.
2. Sauté onion in margarine until tender.
3. Stir in tomato sauce, oregano and salt; simmer 5 minutes, stirring occasionally. Set aside.
4. Brown eggplant slices in remaining margarine.
5. Spread ¼ cup prepared tomato sauce in bottom of shallow 2-quart casserole.
6. Place half the eggplant slices in casserole, top with half of the remaining tomato sauce, sprinkle with 1½ teaspoons Parmesan cheese, and top with half of mozzarella cheese slices.
7. Repeat with remaining ingredients. Bake in preheated 375° F. oven 30 minutes, or until bubbly and cheese on top is golden brown.

Maccheroni all 'Italiana
(Macaroni, Italian Style)

Serves 4

1¼ cups butter
3 tablespoons bread crumbs
¾ pound macaroni, cooked al dente and drained
1⅓ cups tomato pulp
1½ cups tomato juice
1¼ cups plus 2 tablespoons freshly grated Parmesan or Romano cheese

¾ pound smoked ham, cubed
1½ cups fresh mushrooms, diced
1 large onion, finely chopped
1 teaspoon salt
¼ teaspoon freshly ground black pepper
3 eggs, beaten
1½ cups half-and-half
2 tablespoons sweet butter

1. Butter a 9-inch square casserole lightly; top with scant tablespoon bread crumbs.
2. Put in a layer of macaroni, then a layer of tomato pulp and juice, butter, cheese, ham, some of the mushrooms and onion, salt and pepper.
3. Repeat layers until casserole is ¾ full.
4. Combine eggs and cream; pour over macaroni mixture, loosening with fork to allow liquid to seep down through layers.
5. Top with grated cheese, sweet butter and remaining bread crumbs.
6. Bake in preheated 350° F. oven 40 minutes, or until nice and bubbly. Serve for luncheon or supper.

Layered Italian Casserole

Serves 4

1 pound lean ground beef
½ cup onion, chopped
1 small clove garlic, minced
2 cans (8 ounces each) tomato sauce
2 tablespoons parsley, chopped
1¼ teaspoons salt

½ teaspoon oregano
1 package (8 ounces) spaghetti,
  cooked and drained
2 cups ricotta or cottage cheese
8 ounces mozzarella cheese, sliced
½ cup Parmesan cheese, grated

1. Brown beef, onion and garlic in skillet; drain fat.
2. Stir in tomato sauce, parsley, salt and oregano.
3. In a greased 8 x 12-inch shallow baking dish, layer the spaghetti, meat sauce, ricotta and mozzarella.
4. Top with Parmesan cheese.
5. Bake in preheated 350° F. oven for 20 minutes, or until cheese is brown and bubbly.

Parmigiana di Zucchini e Formaggio
(Zucchini & Cheese Casserole)

Serves 6 to 8

1 cup dry bread crumbs
1 cup grated Parmesan cheese
1 clove garlic
1 teaspoon dried basil leaves
½ teaspoon dried oregano leaves
¼ teaspoon pepper
3 large zucchini, sliced

4 eggs
½ to ¾ cup olive oil
3 cups ricotta cheese
¼ cup minced fresh parsley
½ teaspoon salt
2½ cups prepared spaghetti sauce
2 cups shredded mozzarella cheese

1. Combine bread crumbs, Parmesan cheese, garlic, basil, oregano and pepper in blender. Blend 20 seconds.
2. Set aside ⅔ cup crumbs.
3. Dip zucchini slices in 1 beaten egg; coat with crumbs.
4. Sauté zucchini in olive oil in large skillet until golden. Drain.
5. Mix ricotta with remaining eggs, parsley and salt.
6. Spread ½ of spaghetti sauce in a 13 x 9-inch baking pan.
7. Layer with ⅓ of zucchini, ½ of ricotta mixture and ⅓ of mozzarella.
8. Repeat layers, ending with remaining spaghetti sauce and mozzarella.
9. Sprinkle with reserved crumbs.
10. Bake in preheated 350° F. oven 1 hour.
11. Let stand 10 minutes before cutting into squares.

NOTE: This is an award-winning recipe!

Italian Eggs & Asparagus

Serves 2 to 3

1 pound fresh asparagus,
   carefully cleaned and cut into
   2-inch pieces
¼ cup fine-grade olive oil
1 cup chopped mild onion
½ cup chicken stock

½ cup grated Sardo or Parmesan
   cheese
1 teaspoon dried basil
salt to taste
white pepper to taste
6 large eggs

1. Sauté asparagus in oil in skillet over medium heat, turning often.
2. When asparagus begins to brown, add onions and cook over medium heat until onion softens.
3. Add chicken stock; simmer 5 minutes.
4. Add cheese, basil, salt and white pepper to taste. Cover and simmer 5 minutes longer, or until sauce thickens slightly.
5. Drop eggs, one at a time, into skillet on top of asparagus (keeping yolks intact). Cover and simmer until whites set. (Be careful not to overcook the eggs.)
6. Serve piping hot with additional grated cheese, if desired. Great for luncheon or supper dish!

Mozzarella en Carrozza
(Fried Mozzarella Sandwich)

Serves 4

8 slices white bread
1 pound mozzarella, thinly sliced
seasoned flour
2 eggs, beaten with 2 tablespoons
   skim milk

olive oil
salt
pepper
lemon wedges

1. Trim crusts from bread.
2. Place mozzarella slices between slices of bread; cut into triangles.
3. Dredge sandwiches in seasoned flour; dip in egg-milk mixture.
4. Fill skillet with 1 inch olive oil; heat 2 to 3 minutes.
5. Fry sandwiches 2 to 3 minutes per side, or until golden.
6. Drain well on paper towels. Serve at once with salt, pepper and lemon wedges.

NOTE: If desired, bread can be briefly soaked in milk before adding cheese. This is a favorite snack with Neopolitans who like to eat the sizzling sandwich with a light Italian beer.

Mama's Spinach Ricotta Roll

Serves 6

1 package frozen chopped spinach
salt to taste
pepper to taste
nutmeg to taste
1 pound ricotta cheese
½ cup finely grated Parmesan
   cheese
2 tablespoons chopped fresh
   parsley
3 egg whites

1 cup all-purpose flour
1⅓ cups water
olive oil
1 medium onion, chopped
1 clove garlic, chopped
2 cans (1 pound each) Italian plum
   tomatoes, coarsely chopped
1 teaspoon basil
1 teaspoon oregano
½ bay leaf

1. Thaw spinach and squeeze dry with hands. Season with salt, pepper and nutmeg to taste; set aside.
2. Mix ricotta with ½ cup Parmesan cheese and 1 tablespoon chopped parsley. Season with salt, pepper and nutmeg to taste; set aside.
3. Prepare crêpes by mixing together egg whites, flour and water. Beat with wire whisk to get rid of lumps. Strain through fine sieve; set aside.
4. Heat several tablespoons olive oil in bottom of saucepan (enough to coat bottom of pan).
5. Add onion and cook until transparent.
6. Add garlic and tomatoes; simmer 30 minutes.
7. Add remaining parsley, basil, oregano and bay leaf; simmer 30 minutes longer.
8. While marinara sauce cooks, prepare crêpes:
   a. Lightly coat 6-inch crêpe pan with olive oil.
   b. Ladle 2½ tablespoons crêpe batter into heated pan, tilting pan to cover evenly.
   c. When edges of crêpe turns lacy and brown, turn crêpe and brown other side.
   d. Remove crêpe and place on platter. Continue until all the batter is used, re-oiling crêpe pan when necessary.
9. When crêpes are done and sauce is ready, assemble crêpes:
   a. Spoon 2 rounded tablespoons ricotta mixture and 1 tablespoon spinach mixture on each crêpe.
   b. Fold or roll crêpes up to seal in mixture.
   c. Place rolled crêpes in greased rectangular casserole.
10. When casserole is filled, spoon marinara sauce over top to cover.
11. Bake in preheated 325° F. oven 15 to 20 minutes.
12. Serve with additional freshly grated Parmesan cheese. Allow 2 crêpes per person.

Pomodori Ripeni con Funghi e Uove
(Tomatoes Stuffed with Mushrooms and Eggs)

Serves 6

6 firm tomatoes
1 teaspoon salt
¼ teaspoon freshly ground black
  pepper
¾ pound fresh mushrooms
4 tablespoons butter or
  margarine
4 eggs, beaten

¾ cup cubed cooked ham
  or prosciutto (1 pound)
½ chopped onion
1 small clove garlic, minced
chopped fresh parsley
scant teaspoon oregano
  leaves, crushed
1 tablespoon dry bread crumbs

1. Cut off tops from tomatoes; scoop out centers carefully (reserve pulp to use in soups and/or salads). Turn tomatoes upside down to drain.
2. Sprinkle insides with ½ teaspoon salt and ⅛ teaspoon black pepper.
3. Arrange tomatoes on greased baking pan. Bake in preheated 350° F. oven 5 minutes to soften; remove from oven.
4. Rinse, pat-dry, and slice mushrooms; set aside.
5. Melt 1 tablespoon butter in skillet.
6. Add eggs and remaining salt to skillet. Cook, stirring, until eggs firm up slightly.
7. Transfer eggs to bowl; cover to keep eggs warm.
8. Melt 2 tablespoons butter in skillet; add ham, onion, garlic, 1 tablespoon parsley, oregano, remaining salt, pepper and mushrooms. Sauté until mushrooms are tender.
9. Add reserved eggs to vegetable mixture; heat and stir.
10. Spoon an equal amount of filling into each tomato.
11. Stir bread crumbs into remaining melted butter; sprinkle over tops.
12. Bake in preheated 350° F. oven about 5 minutes, or until golden.
13. Garnish with additional parsley.

NOTE: This dish is native to Tuscany.

Fried Mozzarella Marinara

Serves 6 to 8

1 brick mozzarella cheese
  (whole-milk mozzarella is
  best)
little milk
seasoned flour

fine bread crumbs
olive oil
marinara sauce (homemade or
  canned)
anchovy fillets (optional garnish)

1. Cut mozzarella into ½-inch thick rectangles or squares.
2. Dip cheese slices into milk, then seasoned flour, milk again, and finally in bread crumbs.
3. Pour olive oil ¼-inch deep in large skillet and heat.
4. Brown cheese quickly in hot olive oil; turn and brown on reverse side.
5. Remove cheese carefully with spatula to plate.
6. Put a dollop of marinara sauce over each cheese slice.
7. Garnish with 2 anchovy fillets, if desired.

Calamari Neopolitana

Serves 4

2 to 3 pounds whole squid,
  fresh or frozen
¼ cup olive oil
2 large cloves garlic, minced
1 tablespoon fresh lemon juice

⅛ teaspoon dill weed
salt to taste
pepper to taste
1 cup dry white wine
2 cups hot cooked rice

1. Thaw frozen squid and clean. Reserve tentacles. Cut squid into ¾-inch rings and tentacles into 1-inch pieces.
2. Sauté squid in hot oil for a few minutes.
3. Add garlic, lemon juice, dill weed, salt, pepper, and wine.
4. Cover and simmer 45 minutes, or until tender.
5. Serve with hot cooked rice.

Cioppino
(Fish Stew)

Serves 4 to 6

¼ cup salad oil
1 cup chopped onion
1 cup chopped green pepper
½ cup chopped parsley
4 cloves garlic, minced
1 can (16 ounces) tomatoes
2 cans (8 ounces each)
  tomato sauce
2 bay leaves
1 teaspoon salt
¼ teaspoon dried leaf thyme

¼ teaspoon dried leaf marjoram
½ to ¾ teaspoon Tabasco
  sauce
1½ cups dry white wine
1 pound halibut steaks or other
  firm white fish, cut into
  1-inch cubes
1 pound fresh or frozen shrimp,
  shelled and deveined
1 can (10 ounces) whole clams,
  drained

1. Heat oil in large saucepan.
2. Add onion, green pepper, parsley and garlic; cook until tender.
3. Add tomatoes, tomato sauce, bay leaves, salt, thyme, marjoram and Tabasco sauce. Simmer, covered, 2 hours, stirring occasionally.
4. Add wine; cook, uncovered, 10 minutes.
5. Add halibut and shrimp. Cover and simmer 15 minutes, or until fish and shrimp are cooked.
6. Add drained clams and heat.
7. Serve in soup plates.

NOTE: This aromatic dish is an invention of Italian fishermen in San Francisco. Supposedly, they put the leftovers of the day's catch into a big pot, stewed it with tomatoes, oil, garlic and seasonings, and came up with what we know as "cioppini." Others claim the first savory pot was concocted by an Italian named Guiseppe Buzzaro, who owned a restaurant on a boat anchored off the famed Fisherman's Wharf.

Brodetto
(Fish Stew)

Serves 4 to 6

⅓ cup chopped green pepper
⅓ cup chopped onion
1 large clove garlic, minced
1 small bay leaf
1 teaspoon basil leaves,
   crushed
½ teaspoon oregano leaves,
   crushed
½ teaspoon thyme leaves,
   crushed

2 tablespoons olive oil
½ cup dry red Italian wine
1 can (10¾ ounces) condensed
   chicken broth
1 can (11 ounces) condensed
   tomato bisque soup
1 soup can water
¼ cup chopped parsley
1 pound fillets of white fish, cut
   in 2-inch pieces

½ pound medium shrimp, shelled

1. Cook green pepper and onion in olive oil in skillet with garlic, bay leaf, basil, oregano and thyme until tender.
2. Add wine; simmer 2 minutes.
3. Add remaining ingredients. Bring to a boil.
4. Reduce heat, cover, and simmer 10 minutes, or until done, stirring gently now and then.
5. Remove bay leaf and serve.

NOTE: This tasty fish stew comes from the eastern coast of Italy where fish is very plentiful. The fish is adjusted to what is available in the United States, but the flavor is pure Italian!

Pesce con Vino e Salsa Verde
(Poached Fish with Wine & Green Sauce)

Serves 4

1 bottle (8 ounces) clam juice
1 cup water
½ cup dry white wine
8 celery leaves
¼ teaspoon ground pepper
2 pounds sole or turbot fillets
3 tablespoons fresh lemon juice

3 hard-cooked eggs, quartered
10 sprigs parsley
3 tablespoons chopped green
   onions
2 cloves garlic
⅛ teaspoon salt
½ cup olive oil

1. Heat clam juice, water, wine, celery leaves and pepper to boiling in large skillet.
2. Reduce heat; simmer 10 minutes.
3. Add fish to skillet; simmer, covered, until tender, about 5 minutes.
4. Remove to platter with spatula.
5. Place remaining ingredients except oil in blender; blend until smooth.
6. Add oil gradually.
7. Serve sauce over fish.

Gamberi Marinara
(Marinated Shrimp)

Serves 6 to 8

1½ pounds cooked shrimp
  in shells
½ cup olive oil
¼ cup spaghetti sauce
2 tablespoons horseradish mustard
½ cup minced celery
½ cup green onions, minced

½ cup drained capers
1 clove garlic, minced
1½ teaspoons paprika
½ teaspoon salt
dash cayenne pepper
shredded lettuce
lemon wedges (for garnish)

1. Peel cooked shrimp, leaving tails on.
2. Mix remaining ingredients, except lettuce and lemon in mixing bowl; stir in shrimp.
3. Refrigerate, covered, 12 hours, stirring 2 or 3 times.
4. Spoon onto lettuce-lined plate; garnish with lemon.

Red Snapper in Tomato Sauce Italian

Serves 4

2 pounds red snapper, grouper
  or sea bass
¼ cup olive oil
1 clove garlic, slivered
red pepper flakes (to taste)

½ cup chopped tomato
  (fresh preferably)
salt
¼ cup dry white wine
chopped fresh parsley (for garnish)

1. Clean fish; set aside.
2. Heat oil in skillet; add fish, garlic, red pepper, tomato, and salt to taste.
3. Cover and cook gently 10 minutes.
4. Add wine; cover and cook until fish is tender.
5. Serve piping hot, garnished with chopped fresh parsley.

NOTE: Romans cook this with a piece of dried hot red pepper, but red pepper flakes work very well.

Fillet of Sole Italienne

Serves 6

¼ cup chopped onion
2 cups sliced fresh mushrooms
2 tablespoons 100% corn oil
  margarine
2 pounds sole fillets

2 tablespoons fresh lemon juice
1 tablespoon chopped parsley
1 teaspoon oregano
⅛ teaspoon freshly ground
  black pepper

1. Sauté onions and mushrooms in margarine in large skillet until tender.
2. Lay sole fillets in pan and sprinkle remaining ingredients over fish.
3. Cover and simmer gently 20 minutes. (Do not overcook fish.)
4. Serve at once.

Pesce al Forno con Funghi
(Baked Fish with Mushrooms)

Serves 4 to 6

¾ pound fresh mushrooms
¼ cup butter
¾ cup sliced scallions
½ teaspoon minced garlic
3 teaspoons fresh lemon juice

1 teaspoon salt
⅛ teaspoon ground black pepper
2 pounds flounder fillets
2 tablespoons soft bread crumbs
1 teaspoon freshly grated Parmesan cheese

1. Wash, pat-dry, and slice mushrooms (makes about 4 cups).
2. Melt 2 tablespoons butter in large skillet.
3. Add mushrooms, scallions, garlic, 1 teaspoon lemon juice, salt and black pepper; cook 5 minutes.
4. Transfer mushroom mixture with slotted spoon to a 2-quart baking pan.
5. Roll fish fillets; place side by side on top of mushrooms.
6. Melt remaining butter in small saucepan; stir in remaining lemon juice. Pour over fish.
7. Sprinkle fish with bread crumbs and cheese.
8. Bake, uncovered, in preheated 350° F. oven until fish flakes easily when tested with a fork, about 20 minutes.
9. Garnish with additional scallions, if desired.

Ocean Perch, Italian Style

Serves 6

2 pounds ocean perch fillets, fresh or frozen
2 cups sliced onion
2 tablespoons margarine or corn oil
1 can (1 pound) tomatoes
1½ teaspoons salt
1 teaspoon basil

½ teaspoon oregano
½ teaspoon sugar (optional)
3 cups cooked rice
1 package (10 ounces) frozen peas, thawed
½ cup freshly grated or shredded Parmesan or Romano cheese

1. Thaw fish if frozen. Slice fillets into 1½-inch pieces; set aside.
2. Sauté onion in margarine until tender, but not brown.
3. Add tomatoes, salt, basil, oregano and sugar; stir. Simmer, uncovered, 10 minutes. Add fillets, mixing carefully.
4. Combine rice, peas and ¼ cup cheese; mix well.
5. Spoon into shallow 2-quart casserole, making a layer on bottom and up sides of casserole. Spoon fish-vegetable mixture into center.
6. Cover casserole with aluminum foil. Bake in preheated 375° F. oven 25 minutes.
7. Uncover and sprinkle with remaining cheese.
8. Bake 5 minutes longer, or until cheese is softened and fish flakes easily when tested with a fork.

Sogliole alla Marinara
(Fried Pickled Sole)
Serves 6

2½ pounds sole or flounder
  (each weighing about ¾ pound)
⅓ cup all-purpose flour
1 teaspoon salt
freshly ground black pepper
⅓ cup fine-grade olive oil

3 cups onions, chopped
3 tablespoons seedless raisins
  chopped
3 tablespoons pine nuts or
  chopped almonds
⅔ cup vinegar

1. Clean and dry fish. Remove head but leave body whole.
2. Combine flour with salt and pepper on a plate.
3. Roll fish in seasoned flour.
4. Heat oil in skillet; add onions and fry until golden.
5. Remove onions to hot plate.
6. Place fish, raisins and pine nuts in oil. Fry fish until golden brown on both sides.
7. Remove fish from skillet. Return onions to skillet.
8. Add vinegar to mixture; heat thoroughly.
9. Put fish into a deep dish; cover with vinegar mixture, so mixture covers the entire fish.
10. Let stand at least 3 to 4 hours before serving.

NOTE: This fish dish is traditionally served on July 19th, at the Feast of Redemption. It is simple to make, and can be used as a dinner appetizer or luncheon offering.

Trout in White Wine, Milanese
Serves 4

1 tablespoon sweet butter
1 tablespoon fine-grade olive oil
1 chopped onion
salt to taste
pepper to taste
2 sprigs parsley
1 small bay leaf, crumbled

1½ cups dry white wine
1 cup water
4 cleaned trout, weighing
  ½ to ¾ pound each
bread croutons, fried in sweet butter
  (for garnish)
lemon slices (for garnish)

1. Heat together butter and olive oil in skillet.
2. Sauté onion in butter-olive oil mixture until limp.
3. Add salt, pepper, parsley, bay leaf, wine and water. Cover and simmer 5 minutes.
4. Add trout; poach fish in covered pan 8 to 10 minutes, or until done. (Poaching liquid should not boil.)
5. Drain trout; remove to heated plates.
6. Serve with a few drops of poaching liquid. Garnish plate with croutons and lemon slices.

NOTE: A dieter's delight! Works well with other small, lean fish.

Sea Bass Sicilian

Serves 6

1 dressed whole sea bass,
  weighing 3 pounds
salt
white pepper
½ teaspoon basil
1 clove garlic, minced
1 cup chopped onions

¼ cup fine-grade olive oil
1 can (10½ ounces) red
  clam sauce
½ cup dry white wine
1 cup pimiento-stuffed olives,
  halved
lemon slices (for garnish)

1. Put fish in foil-lined baking pan.
2. Season to taste with salt and white pepper.
3. Sprinkle basil evenly over top.
4. Sauté garlic and onions in olive oil until limp; pour over fish.
5. Bake in preheated 350° F. oven 20 minutes.
6. Combine clam sauce, wine and olives; pour over fish.
7. Bake 20 minutes longer, or until fish flakes easily with fork. (Do not overcook.)
8. Remove fish from sauce and place on warm platter.
9. Cook sauce over high heat, stirring to reduce in volume slightly.
10. Pour sauce around fish. Garnish with lemon slices.

Shrimp Scampi

Serves 2

12 to 14 medium green shrimp,
  shelled and deveined
3 tablespoons fresh lemon juice
3 cloves garlic, minced
3 shallots, minced
1 tablespoon fresh parsley, chopped
1 teaspoon dried oregano

salt to taste
white pepper to taste
2 cups Soave wine, or any good
  very dry white wine
1 cup cooked rice
parsley sprigs (for garnish)
paprika (for garnish)

1. Sauté shrimps briefly in non-stick pan with lemon juice, or brush lightly with lemon juice and broil briefly.
2. In large skillet add garlic, shallots, parsley, oregano, salt and pepper to wine; simmer 5 minutes.
3. Add shrimp and simmer until white and firm.
4. Remove shrimp and spoon over hot rice (tastier if seasoned with chicken stock and fresh herbs). Keep shrimp and rice warm.
5. Reduce herb-wine liquid to ¼ cup.
6. Pour over shrimp and rice. Garnish with parsley and paprika.

NOTE: Clam juice or chicken broth can be substituted for wine.

Tagliarini al Tonno
(Tagliarini & Tuna)

Serves 4 to 6

2 cans (6½ ounces each)
  chunk light tuna
1 package (8 ounces) tagliarini
  or spaghetti
boiling salted water
1 cup chopped green onion
1 cup chopped green pepper

2 tablespoons minced garlic
1½ teaspoons salt
1 teaspoon oregano, crumbled
1 teaspoon sweet basil, crumbled
½ teaspoon rosemary, crumbled
¾ cup olive oil
½ cup butter

freshly grated Parmesan cheese

1. Drain tuna well.
2. Cook tagliarini in boiling salted water until tender.
3. Sauté onion, pepper, garlic and seasonings in olive oil and butter until green pepper is soft.
4. Fold in tuna.
5. Toss tuna mixture with hot cooked tagliarini. Sprinkle with generous amounts of Parmesan cheese to serve.

Shrimp Cacciatora

Serves 4

1 tablespoon sweet butter
2 tablespoons fine-grade
  olive oil
1 cup chopped onion
1 large clove garlic,
  peeled and halved
2 cups canned Italian
  plum tomatoes

1 green pepper, cut in large dices
½ pound fresh mushrooms,
  sliced
½ cup dry white wine
1½ pounds green shrimp,
  shelled and deveined
hot cooked rice
chopped fresh parsley (optional garnish)

1. Heat butter and olive oil together.
2. Add onion and garlic. Sauté over low heat until onion is golden.
3. Add tomatoes and green pepper; simmer, uncovered, 15 minutes.
4. Add mushrooms and wine; simmer, uncovered, 20 minutes longer, or until sauce thickens.
5. Remove and discard garlic.
6. Add shrimp; simmer in tomato sauce until shrimp turn pink, 10 to 15 minutes.
7. Spoon shrimp mixture over hot cooked rice. If desired, garnish with chopped fresh parsley.

Pollo alla Cacciatore
(Hunter-Style Chicken)

Serves 6

2 tablespoons olive oil
2 broiler-fryer chickens, weighing 2½ to 3 pounds each, cut into eighths
½ cup onion flakes
1 teaspoon instant minced garlic
⅓ cup water
1 can (1 pound 12 ounces) tomatoes, broken up

1 can (6 ounces) tomato paste
1½ teaspoons oregano leaves, crumbled
3 small bay leaves
1 teaspoon salt
¼ teaspoon ground black pepper
½ cup dry white wine
spaghetti or noodles

1. Heat oil in Dutch oven. Add chicken, a few pieces at a time, and brown well on all sides.
2. Meanwhile, rehydrate onion flakes and minced garlic in water for 10 minutes.
3. Add onion and garlic to Dutch oven; sauté 5 minutes.
4. Return all of chicken to Dutch oven. Add tomatoes, tomato paste, oregano, bay leaves, salt and black pepper; mix gently.
5. Cover and simmer 45 minutes, or until chicken is tender.
6. Remove chicken to serving platter and cover with foil to keep warm.
7. Add wine to sauce in Dutch oven; simmer, uncovered, 10 minutes.
8. Remove bay leaves. Spoon sauce over chicken. Serve with spaghetti or noodles.

Chicken Saltimbocca

Serves 6

3 whole chicken breasts, split, skinned and boned (1½ pounds boneless)
¼ teaspoon rubbed sage
6 thin slices prosciutto or boiled ham (4 ounces)

¼ cup flour
¼ cup butter or margarine
½ cup Marsala wine
1 can (10¾ ounces) condensed chicken broth

1. Flatten chicken breasts with flat side of knife; rub with sage.
2. Top each with sliced prosciutto; secure with toothpicks. Dust with flour.
3. Brown in butter in skillet.
4. Add wine; bring to boil, stirring to loosen browned bits.
5. Add chicken broth; bring to boil.
6. Reduce heat; simmer 5 minutes, or until sauce is slightly thickened.

NOTE: Traditionally, saltimbocca is made with veal, but boneless chicken breasts work very well.

Tony's Chicken Marengo

Serves 4

1 broiler-fryer chicken,
  cut into serving pieces
2 tablespoons butter
2 tablespoons olive oil
2 onions, peeled and thinly
  sliced
1½ tablespoons flour
1 can (16 ounces) tomatoes,
  drained and cut into chunks
2 tablespoons tomato paste
1 cup chicken broth

½ cup dry white wine
1 to 2 fresh cloves garlic,
  peeled and finely minced
1 teaspoon crushed oregano
½ pound fresh mushrooms,
  thickly sliced
½ cup pitted black olive
herb salt to taste
pepper to taste
3 tablespoons chopped parsley
1 teaspoon grated lemon rind

hot cooked rice or buttered noodles

1. Sauté chicken in butter and olive oil in large skillet or Dutch oven until lightly browned.
2. Push chicken to sides of pan and sauté onion until golden. Drain off excess grease.
3. Sprinkle onions with flour; add tomatoes, tomato paste, chicken broth, wine, garlic and oregano.
4. Mix with chicken; cover and simmer 30 minutes.
5. Stir in mushrooms and olives; cover and simmer 15 minutes longer.
6. Season to taste with herb salt and pepper.
7. Transfer to a heated platter and sprinkle with parsley and grated lemon rind.
8. Serve over hot cooked rice or hot buttered noodles.

Low-Sodium Chicken Marengo

Serves 4

1 broiler-fryer chicken, cut up
¼ cup unsalted margarine
⅛ teaspoon freshly ground
  black pepper
½ pound pearl onions, peeled
½ pound mushrooms, sliced

1 can (16 ounces) low-sodium
  tomatoes
½ cup dry white wine
4 teaspoons flour
2 tablespoons chopped fresh
  parsley (for garnish)

1. Remove loose skin and visible fat from chicken pieces.
2. Heat margarine in Dutch oven.
3. Sprinkle chicken generously with pepper; brown in hot margarine. Remove from pan.
4. Put onions and mushrooms in skillet; cook and stir until lightly browned.
5. Mix in tomatoes and ¼ cup wine.
6. Return chicken to pan and bring liquid to a boil.
7. Reduce heat, cover, and simmer 30 minutes, or until chicken is tender.
8. Remove chicken to hot platter.
9. Blend together flour and remaining wine; stir into liquid in skillet. Simmer 1 minute, or until slightly thickened.
10. Pour sauce over chicken and garnish with chopped parsley to serve.

Mediterranean Chicken Breasts

Serves 8

2 lemons
4 large cloves garlic, minced
1½ teaspoons salt
1 teaspoon chopped fresh oregano
¼ teaspoon freshly ground
  black pepper
¼ cup olive oil
¼ cup safflower oil
4 chicken breasts, boned,
  skinned, and cut in half

1 cup freshly grated Parmesan cheese
1 cup fine, white fresh bread crumbs
2 cups chicken stock
30 to 40 garlic cloves, peeled
butter
1 cup dry white wine
⅓ cup minced fresh parsley leaves
parsley sprigs (for garnish)

1. Remove lemon zest (yellow part of peel) with vegetable peeler and mince.
2. With wide-blade knife, make paste of minced garlic and salt.
3. Combine lemon zest, 2 tablespoons lemon juice, garlic paste, oregano, pepper and oil.
   Alternate 1. Place unminced zest and garlic cloves in food processor. Using steel blade, process a few seconds.
   Alternate 2. Add salt, pepper, oregano leaves and lemon juice. With processor turned on, add oils in slow stream.
4. Coat chicken breasts with marinade and scrape off excess.
5. Roll meat in mixture of Parmesan and bread crumbs. Lay coated breasts on waxed paper; allow to set 15 minutes to several hours.
6. Heat chicken stock to boiling and blanch garlic cloves in stock 10 minutes.
7. Remove garlic; reserve stock for sauce by heating until volume is reduced to 1½ cups.
8. Place breasts in buttered shallow baking dish. Drizzle a little melted butter on each breast. Strew blanched garlic cloves over and around breasts.
9. Cover with foil and bake in preheated 375° F. oven 15 to 20 minutes, or until done.
10. Remove foil and run chicken under broiler until golden.
11. Remove to heated platter and distribute garlic around breasts. Keep warm while sauce cooks.
12. Add wine to pan juices in baking pan; deglaze pan over high heat, scraping any brown bits clinging to bottom and sides of pan.
13. Pour mixture into saucepan; reduce liquid over high heat to ¼ cup.
14. Add reserved chicken stock and parsley leaves; reduce mixture to 1 cup over medium heat, stirring.
15. Remove pan from heat. Add lemon juice, salt and pepper to taste.
16. Pour sauce over breasts and garnish platter with parsley sprigs.

NOTE: Highly aromatic and delicious!

Chicken Parmigiana

Serves 6

6 boneless, skinned chicken
  breast halves
salt
pepper
dried oregano leaves, crumbled
2 teaspoons Angostura
  aromatic bitters

1 egg
2 cups cornflake crumbs
¼ cup butter or margarine
¼ cup olive or corn oil
1½ cups marinara or pizza sauce
8 ounces mozzarella cheese, cut into
  6 slices

1. Sprinkle chicken breasts with salt, pepper and oregano.
2. Beat together Angostura and egg.
3. Dip chicken breasts into egg, then into crumbs. Press crumbs firmly to make them stick.
4. Heat butter and oil together in large skillet. Brown chicken breasts slowly on all sides.
5. Place breasts in a single layer on a shallow pan. Top with sauce and mozzarella slices.
6. Bake in preheated 350° F. oven 20 minutes, or until cheese is melted.
7. Serve hot with spaghetti mixed with butter and grated Parmesan cheese.

Italian-Style Stuffed Duckling

Serves 4

1 frozen duckling, weighing
  4½ to 5 pounds, defrosted
1 clove garlic
¾ teaspoon salt
½ pound pork sausage meat
1 cup diced celery
½ cup coarsely chopped onion

1 tablespoon olive or corn oil
3½ cups ½-inch bread cubes
½ cup sliced pitted black olives
½ teaspoon rosemary
1 teaspoon oregano
2 tablespoons sherry (optional)
¼ cup shredded Parmesan cheese

1. Wash and drain duckling; dry skin gently with paper toweling.
2. Rub body cavity with cut surface of garlic clove. Sprinkle body and neck cavities with ½ teaspoon salt.
3. Cook sausage meat, celery and onion in oil until celery is tender, but not brown, and meat is crumbly. Drain off excess fat.
4. Add bread cubes, olives, remaining salt, seasonings and sherry; toss gently.
5. Fill neck and body cavities loosely with stuffing. Skewer neck skin to back, cover opening of body cavity with aluminum foil, and tie legs together loosely.
6. Place on rack in shallow roasting pan. Bake in preheated 325° F. oven until meat on drumsticks is tender, about 3 hours.
7. Sprinkle cheese over duck during last 15 minutes of roasting.

NOTE: Serve with an Italian salad of red onions, Boston Bibb lettuce, crispy bread sticks and a garnish of cherry tomatoes.

Broiled Chicken Calabrese

Serves 4

1 cleaned broiler-fryer chicken,
weighing 2½ to 3 pounds,
quartered
2 cloves garlic, minced
½ teaspoon salt

⅛ teaspoon paprika
freshly ground black pepper
dash cayenne
3 tablespoons minced parsley
⅓ cup fine-grade olive oil

1. Wash and dry chicken quarters.
2. Mash garlic, salt, paprika, pepper and cayenne together with a spoon.
3. Rub this mixture into chicken and let stand 30 minutes.
4. Arrange chicken quarters on broiler rack, skin-side up.
5. Sprinkle with parsley and additional paprika; brush with some of the oil.
6. Broil in preheated broiler 5 minutes; turn, brush with remaining oil, and broil 10 minutes.
7. Turn again; broil 5 minutes longer, or until chicken is fork-tender.

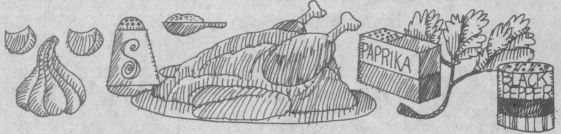

Roasted Cornish Hens al Barolo

Serves 3 to 6

3 rock Cornish hens, each
weighing about 1½ pounds
¾ teaspoon salt
3 green onions
½ lemon, cut into thirds
¼ cup butter or margarine

1 clove garlic, split
½ teaspoon rosemary leaves,
crumbled
1 cup Barolo red wine,
approximately
watercress (for garnish)

1. Sprinkle each hen inside and out with salt.
2. Place 1 onion and piece of lemon inside each hen; tie legs together.
3. Arrange hens in shallow roasting pan.
4. Melt butter in small saucepan; add garlic, rosemary and ½ cup red wine. Brush over hens.
5. Roast hens, uncovered, in preheated 400° F. oven, brushing often with remaining sauce until hens are golden (about 45 minutes).
6. Transfer to heated platter; remove strings. Keep warm.
7. Pour drippings into 1-cup measuring cup.
8. Skim off excess fat; add red wine to make 1 cup.
9. Pour into small saucepan; bring to a boil. Serve with hens.
10. Garnish with watercress and additional lemon. Serve with Savory Risotto, if desired.

Chicken Italiano

Serves 4 to 6

2 pounds chicken parts
2 tablespoons olive oil
1 can (10½ ounces) condensed
  chicken broth
½ cup chopped tomatoes
1 onion, peeled and chopped
¼ teaspoon dried oregano

¼ teaspoon basil leaves
¼ teaspoon salt
freshly ground black
  pepper to taste
¼ cup flour
⅓ cup water
cooked rice

chopped fresh parsley (for garnish)

1. Brown chicken in olive oil; pour off excess fat.
2. Add broth, tomatoes, onion, oregano, basil, salt and pepper.
3. Cover and simmer 45 minutes, or until chicken is tender.
4. Blend flour into water to form smooth paste.
5. Slowly stir paste into chicken mixture; cook until gravy is thickened.
6. Serve with rice; garnish with parsley.

Baked Chicken Italiano

Serves 4

½ cup grated Parmesan cheese
2 tablespoons minced parsley
1 teaspoon oregano leaves
¼ teaspoon crushed fresh
  garlic

dash ground black pepper
2 whole chicken breasts, boned,
  skinned and split
3 tablespoons diet imitation
  margarine, melted

1. Combine Parmesan cheese, parsley, oregano, garlic and pepper; mix well.
2. Dip chicken breasts in melted margarine, then into cheese mixture to coat well.
3. Place in a large shallow baking dish. Drizzle any remaining margarine over chicken breasts.
4. Bake in preheated 375° F. oven 25 minutes, or until chicken is tender. Serve at once.

Pollo alla Cacciatore

Serves 4

2 pounds chicken parts
3 tablespoons flour
2 tablespoons olive oil
1 can (11 ounces) condensed
  tomato bisque soup
⅓ cup Chianti or other dry red wine

½ cup sliced onion
1 cup sliced fresh mushrooms
  (about ¾ pound)
½ teaspoon basil leaves, crushed
1 small bay leaf
1 small green pepper, cut in strips

1. Dust chicken with flour; brown in hot oil in skillet.
2. Add soup, wine, onion, mushrooms and seasonings; cover and cook over low heat 30 minutes.
3. Add green pepper; cook 15 minutes more, or until done, stirring occasionally.
4. Remove bay leaf and serve.

Involtini di Bistecche

Serves 6

1½ pounds thinly sliced round
  steak (about ¼ inch thick)
¼ pound ground veal
1 egg, slightly beaten
¼ cup small bread crumbs
2 tablespoons grated Parmesan
  cheese
2 slices (2 ounces) salami,
  cut in strips
2 hard-cooked eggs, sliced

2 slices provolone cheese, cut
  in strips (2 ounces)
2 tablespoons shortening
1 can (10¾ ounces) condensed
  tomato soup
¼ cup water
¼ cup dry red Italian wine
½ cup chopped onion
1 clove garlic, minced
1 small bay leaf

1. Pound steak.
2. Combine veal, egg, bread crumbs and Parmesan cheese.
3. Spread mixture evenly on steak to within 1 inch of edges.
4. Press sliced egg, salami and provolone cheese into meat mixture.
5. Starting at narrow end, roll up steak and tuck in ends. Tie with string or fasten with skewers.
6. Brown steak roll in shortening in skillet; pour off fat.
7. Add remaining ingredients. Cover and cook over low heat 1 hour.
8. Turn; cook 1 hour more, or until done, stirring occasionally.
9. Remove bay leaf and serve.

Italian Beef Cubes

Serves 4

2 tablespoons unsifted flour
dash ground black pepper
1 pound beef cubes
3 tablespoons unsalted margarine
2 cups coarsely chopped
  fresh tomatoes
1 cup sliced onion

⅓ cup chopped green pepper
2 cans (12 ounces each) low-sodium
  tomato juice
½ cup water
½ cup Chianti
1 package (8 ounces) spaghetti
¼ cup minced fresh parsley

1. Combine flour and black pepper; coat beef cubes with mixture.
2. Melt margarine in Dutch oven over medium heat; add beef cubes and brown on all sides.
3. Mix in tomatoes, onion, green pepper, tomato juice, water and wine.
4. Bring to a boil over medium high heat.
5. Reduce heat to low, cover, and simmer 1½ hours, stirring occasionally, or until meat is tender.
6. Cook spaghetti according to package directions without using salt. Drain well.
7. Serve prepared beef sauce over hot cooked spaghetti and garnish with chopped spaghetti.

NOTE: Designed for anyone on a low-sodium diet (100 mg. per serving).

Italian Round Steak Roulade

Serves 6

1 beef round steak, cut ½ inch thick, weighing 2 to 2½ pounds
½ pound fresh pork sausage
1 package (10 ounces) frozen chopped spinach, thawed and well drained
¼ cup freshly grated Parmesan cheese
4 to 5 tablespoons flour
1 teaspoon salt
⅛ teaspoon freshly ground black pepper
1 tablespoon olive oil
1 tablespoon butter
1 medium onion, minced
1 clove garlic, minced
⅓ cup water
¾ teaspoon Italian seasoning
1 can (15 ounces) tomato sauce

1. Remove bone from round steak; set aside.
2. Cook sausage in skillet until meat turns white; pour off drippings.
3. Add spinach and Parmesan cheese, mixing lightly.
4. Combine 3 tablespoons flour, salt and pepper; dredge round steak in flour mixture, then pound meat to ¼-inch thickness.
5. Spread pork mixture evenly over surface of meat. Starting at the narrow end, roll steak, jelly-roll fashion; tie securely with string at 1-inch intervals.
6. Brown meat quickly in olive oil and butter in large skillet.
7. Remove meat and pour off all but 1 tablespoon meat drippings.
8. Sauté onion and garlic in drippings until tender.
9. Return meat to skillet; add ⅓ cup water and sprinkle Italian seasoning over meat.
10. Cover tightly and cook slowly 1½ hours.
11. Combine tomato sauce and remaining flour; stir into cooking liquid.
12. Continue cooking, covered, 30 minutes longer, or until meat is tender.
13. Remove meat to heated serving platter. Slice and serve with sauce and spaghetti.

Arrosto di Agnello con Patate
(Roast Spring Lamb with Potatoes)

Serves 6

3 pounds leg of lamb
2 cloves garlic, cut into slivers
1 teaspoon dried rosemary leaves
½ teaspoon dried sage leaves
salt to taste
pepper to taste
2 pounds potatoes, quartered
¼ cup olive oil
¼ cup dry white wine
juice of 1 lemon

1. Make incisions over surface of lamb with sharp knife; insert garlic.
2. Rub lamb with rosemary, sage, salt and pepper.
3. Place in roasting pan. Insert meat thermometer in center of lamb, being careful not to touch bone.
4. Bake in preheated 325° F. oven 1 hour.
5. Remove pan from oven and arrange potatoes around lamb; pour oil and wine over all. Sprinkle with salt and pepper.
6. Return to oven and roast until meat thermometer registers 170° F., about 1 hour.
7. Spoon lemon juice over lamb, then let lamb stand 10 minutes before carving.

Pork Chops Genovese

Serves 4

1 large clove garlic
2 tablespoons fine-grade olive oil
4 loin pork chops, cut ¾ inch
  thick
salt to taste

freshly ground black pepper
  to taste
3 tablespoons tomato paste
¼ cup dry white Italian wine
1 green or red sweet pepper, chopped

½ pound sliced fresh mushrooms

1. Brown garlic in hot olive oil in skillet or Dutch oven.
2. Lift out and discard garlic.
3. Brown chops quickly in garlic-oil on both sides; season lightly with salt and pepper.
4. Dilute tomato paste with wine; add to meat in skillet.
5. Sprinkle sweet pepper and mushrooms over chops.
6. Cover and simmer 45 minutes.

Polpette al Sugo
(Meatballs in Meat Sauce)

Serves 4

1 ounce salt pork, chopped
¼ cup olive oil
1 clove garlic, minced
1½ pounds ground beef
1½ pounds ground pork
4 cups spaghetti sauce
½ cup Chianti

pepper to taste
½ cup grated Parmesan cheese
⅓ cup dry bread crumbs
2 eggs
1 tablespoon minced chives
1 teaspoon dried basil leaves
salt to taste

1. Sauté salt pork in oil in Dutch oven until crisp.
2. Add garlic and ⅓ of meats; sauté until meats are brown.
3. Drain excess fat. Stir in sauce, wine and pepper to taste; heat to boiling.
4. Reduce heat and simmer 20 minutes.
5. Mix remaining ingredients; form into 20 meatballs. Stir into sauce and simmer, covered, 30 minutes.

Calves Liver, Venetian Style

Serves 4

1½ pounds calves liver
¼ cup fine-grade olive oil
½ cup chopped mild white
   onion

¼ cup dry red Italian wine
salt to taste
freshly ground black pepper
   to taste

1. Cut liver into thin strips with sharp knife or scissors.
2. Heat olive oil in skillet; sauté onions in hot oil until golden.
3. Remove onions to warm skillet.
4. Cook liver quickly in oiled skillet.
5. Return onions to skillet; add wine, salt and pepper to taste.
6. Heat through quickly. Serve at once.

Tripe a la Trieste

Serves 6 to 8

2 pounds tripe
¼ cup white vinegar
4 cups water
1 cup onion, chopped
1 large clove garlic, minced

3 sprigs fresh parsley, minced
2 ounces salt pork, chopped
1 cup chicken broth
4 ounces (½ cup) tomato paste
4 ounces mushrooms

⅓ cup freshly grated Parmesan cheese

1. Soak tripe in vinegar-water solution for 1 hour.
2. Drain and cut into julienne strips.
3. Sauté together onion, garlic, parsley and salt pork until onion is limp.
4. Add tripe and stir.
5. Add chicken broth and tomato paste; stir.
6. Add mushrooms and enough fresh water to cover.
7. Cover and simmer 3 hours, stirring often, until tripe is tender and liquid is absorbed.
8. Serve with Parmesan cheese.

Involtini
(Veal Rolls)

Serves 6

6 thin slices veal (about 1 pound)
6 slices prosciutto (about ¼ pound)
12 fresh sage leaves or 1 teaspoon
   dried crumbled sage

¼ cup vegetable oil
salt to taste
1 cup Soave, Pinot Grigio, Lugana
   or other white Italian wine

1. Place veal on board; pound with tenderizing mallet or blunt edge of plate to make slices very thin.
2. Divide each veal slice in two pieces as rectangular as possible; cut prosciutto into 2 rectangles.
3. To assemble, lay ½ slice prosciutto on each veal rectangle; place a sage leaf, or a pinch of dried sage on each center; roll up and fasten with toothpick.
4. Heat oil; add veal rolls and brown over low heat all over. Salt as desired.
5. Add wine. Raise heat to medium; simmer 15 to 20 minutes, or until tender, turning involtini several times during cooking.
6. Remove picks before serving. Arrange on heated serving platter; top with sauce.

Italian Salami-Veal Meat Roll

Serves 8

2 eggs
2 slices Italian bread
½ cup milk
2 tablespoons toasted onion flakes
2 cloves garlic, peeled and minced
1½ teaspoons fresh lemon peel,
   grated
¼ teaspoon ground nutmeg

1 teaspoon salt
freshly ground black pepper
   to taste
2 pounds ground veal
¼ cup parsley, chopped
¼ cup Parmesan cheese, grated
¼ cup pine nuts, chopped
18 slices dry Italian salami

1. In blender container place eggs, bread, milk, onion flakes, garlic, lemon peel, nutmeg, salt and pepper to taste; blend well.
2. Place meat and blended mixture in mixing bowl; mix well with fingers.
3. Lay out meat mixture on sheet of waxed paper, making a 10 x 12-inch rectangle.
4. Lay salami slices on meat, covering evenly. Sprinkle with parsley, cheese and pine nuts.
5. Roll up from the longer side and place, seam-side down, in a buttered baking pan.
6. Bake in preheated 375° F. oven about 45 minutes, or until cooked through.
7. Place on a warmed serving platter. Slice ¾ inch thick.

NOTE: If desired, accompany with a sauce composed of ½ cup each yogurt and dairy sour cream and 2 tablespoons each chopped chives and parsley. Great served hot or cold for buffet or picnic.

Fenella's Osso Buco

Serves 4

4 thick slices veal or beef shin,
  with marrowbone
flour
¼ cup vegetable oil
2 tablespoons butter
1 clove garlic, crushed
2 medium carrots, chopped fine
1 small yellow onion, minced

2 ribs celery, chopped fine
1 cup Barbera, Chianti or other
  red Italian wine
salt to taste
freshly ground black pepper
  to taste
1 bay leaf, crumbled
½ teaspoon thyme

1 to 1½ cups hot beef broth

1. Wash meat and pat dry with paper towels. Dredge with flour and set aside.
2. Heat oil and butter in Dutch oven or large skillet until bubbling.
3. Add garlic and cook until pale brown.
4. Remove garlic; raise heat and add meat.
5. Brown meat quickly on both sides.
6. Add carrots, onion and celery; toss to glaze lightly, about 5 minutes.
7. Add wine; let mixture bubble until nearly evaporated.
8. Lower heat; add seasonings and 1 cup beef broth.
9. Cover and simmer 1½ hours (slightly longer if beef shin is used), turning meat and vegetables from time to time and adding more beef broth as needed.
10. Serve with Italian-style mashed potatoes.

Saltimbocca Milano

Serves 6

3 slices prosciutto ham, cut up
  to fit veal
1½ pounds veal, sliced, pounded thin,
  and cut into 1½ dozen 3-inch-wide
  pieces
3 tablespoons fine-grade olive oil
1 clove fresh garlic

1½ packages (10 ounces each)
  frozen spinach, cooked and
  drained
¾ cup dry white wine
¾ cup beef bouillon
salt to taste
white pepper to taste

1. Place prosciutto on veal pieces, roll up, and secure with toothpicks.
2. Sauté quickly on each side in skillet in olive oil; remove when browned.
3. Sauté garlic and spinach in same oil.
4. Remove garlic and spinach from skillet and place in greased, shallow ovenproof casserole.
5. Arrange veal rolls on top.
6. Pour wine, bouillon and seasonings over all.
7. Bake in preheated 350° F. oven ½ hour, or until veal is tender.

Scaloppine al Limone
(Lemon Veal Scallops)

Serves 2

¾ pound veal scallops
1 tablespoon butter
1 tablespoon olive oil
salt to taste
pepper to taste

3 tablespoons beef broth
3 tablespoons dry white wine
2 tablespoons fresh lemon juice
½ lemon, cut in thin slices
1 tablespoon minced fresh parsley

1. Quickly brown veal in hot butter and olive oil.
2. Add salt and pepper.
3. Add beef broth, wine and lemon juice.
4. Top with lemon slices. Cover and simmer 1 to 2 minutes.
5. Remove to warm serving dishes or platter; top with reduced sauce.
6. Serve with fresh broccoli sautéed in olive oil, butter and a hint of garlic.

Vitella con Riso
(Veal & Rice)

Serves 6

1 small yellow onion, peeled
and thinly sliced
2 tablespoons olive oil
¼ pound Italian pork sausages
(hot or sweet or mixed), cut in
small pieces
2 cups uncooked rice
1 cup canned tomatoes
2 tablespoons chopped fresh parsley
4 cups chicken broth, canned
or homemade

2 tablespoons grated Romano cheese
6 thin veal cutlets, weighing 1½-
1¾ pounds
4 tablespoons sweet butter or
margarine
salt to taste
pepper to taste
¼ cup hot water
parsley (for garnish)

1. Sauté onion in olive oil until limp; add sausages; cook 5 minutes.
2. Add rice; stir mixture.
3. Add tomatoes and parsley; cook, stirring, 5 minutes.
4. Add chicken broth; reduce heat, cover, and cook 25 minutes, or until rice is cooked, stirring often to prevent sticking.
5. Add grated cheese; blend well to make smooth mixture.
6. Fry cutlets quickly in butter until done on both sides; add salt and pepper to taste.
7. When done, remove veal to heated platter.
8. Deglaze pan by adding hot water to skillet. Heat over high heat, scraping brown bits from bottom and sides of pan.
9. Arrange rice on heated platter; top with veal. Pour deglazed gravy over all and garnish with parsley.

Veal Chops Mediterranean

Serves 4

2 tablespoons flour
½ teaspoon salt
⅛ teaspoon pepper
8 small veal loin chops
2 tablespoons cooking oil
1 medium onion, sliced

1 can (10½ ounces) condensed
 beef broth
2 tablespoons fresh lemon juice
½ teaspoon grated lemon peel
1 cup pitted California ripe olives
¼ cup chopped pimiento

2 tablespoons chopped fresh parsley

1. Combine flour, salt and pepper; coat veal chops lightly with flour, reserving remaining flour.
2. Heat oil in skillet; add chops and brown well.
3. Remove chops.
4. Add onion to skillet and cook until transparent.
5. Stir in reserved flour. Add broth and cook, stirring constantly, until sauce boils.
6. Stir in lemon juice and peel.
7. Return chops to skillet. Cover and cook slowly 45 minutes to 1 hour, or until meat is tender.
8. Add ripe olives and pimiento; cook 5 minutes longer.
9. Sprinkle with parsley and serve.

Spezzatino di Vitello alla Salvia
(Veal Stew with Sage)

Serves 6

2 pounds veal cubes for stew
flour
salt
pepper
3 tablespoons olive oil
2 tablespoons butter
4 carrots, sliced

4 ribs celery, sliced
2 small onions, sliced
2 cloves garlic, minced
½ teaspoon dried sage leaves
1 cup dry white wine
1 cup chicken broth
½ pound mushrooms, sliced

cooked green noodles

1. Coat veal with flour; sprinkle with salt and pepper.
2. Sauté veal in oil and butter in Dutch oven until brown; remove.
3. Sauté vegetables and sage 5 minutes.
4. Stir in wine and broth; heat to boiling.
5. Reduce heat; simmer, covered, approximately 45 minutes, or until meat is tender.
6. Stir in mushrooms; simmer 5 minutes.
7. Serve on hot cooked green noodles.

Scaloppine di Vitello al Pomodoro
(Veal Scaloppine in Tomato Sauce)

Serves 4

1 pound veal scallops,
  pounded thin
flour
salt to taste
pepper to taste

2 tablespoons olive oil
2 tablespoons butter
1 cup dry white wine
1 cup spaghetti sauce
½ teaspoon dried oregano leaves

1 tablespoon drained capers

1. Coat veal with flour; sprinkle with salt and pepper.
2. Sauté veal in oil and butter in skillet until brown.
3. Remove and keep warm.
4. Boil remaining ingredients until mixture begins to thicken, about 5 minutes.
5. Spoon sauce over veal.

Vitella con Pepperoni
(Veal & Peppers)

Serves 4 to 6

1½ pounds boneless veal rump, cut
  into 1½-inch cubes
3 tablespoons sweet butter
salt
freshly ground black pepper
1 can (16 ounces) tomatoes

1 onion, sliced
4 large firm green and red peppers
  (2 each or mixed), washed,
  seeded and cut in lengthwise
  strips
4 tablespoons olive oil

⅔ cup dry white Italian wine

1. Brown veal in hot butter in skillet 10 minutes.
2. Season with salt and pepper.
3. Add tomatoes; cover and simmer 30 minutes.
4. Meanwhile, sauté onion and peppers in hot oil 15 minutes, or until tender-crisp, stirring to prevent burning.
5. Add onions and peppers to veal.
6. Add wine; cover and simmer 15 minutes.
7. Serve piping hot alone, or over rice, or with your favorite cooked pasta.

Uccelli Scappati
(Veal Birds)

Serves 4 to 6

1½ pounds boneless veal rump,
   cut into 1½-inch cubes
4 slices lean bacon

pinch rosemary
salt
freshly ground black pepper

1. Skewer veal and bacon alternately until skewers are filled.
2. Sprinkle lightly with rosemary.
3. Place on broiler rack 6 inches below preheated broiler. Broil on each side 5 to 6 minutes, turning until brown or tender.
4. Season to taste with salt and pepper.
5. Serve with pan gravy or thin lemon slices. (Low in calories but delicious eating!)

NOTE: *If desired, pieces of zucchini can be alternated between veal and bacon. Great grilled outdoors!*

Veal Scaloppine

Serves 4

⅓ cup unsalted margarine
½ pound mushrooms, thinly
   sliced
¼ cup flour
⅛ teaspoon freshly ground
   black pepper

1 pound veal cutlets,
   thinly sliced
¼ cup dry sherry
1 tablespoon water
chopped fresh parsley
   (for garnish)

1. Melt margarine in large skillet over medium heat.
2. Sauté mushrooms until tender; remove from pan.
3. Combine flour and pepper; coat veal with flour mixture.
4. Brown veal in remaining margarine, a few pieces at a time, until done; remove from pan.
5. Add sherry and water to skillet, stirring until liquid is slightly thickened.
6. Return veal and mushrooms to pan to heat through.
7. Arrange on a serving platter and garnish with chopped parsley.

Basic Directions for Cooking Artichokes

Wash artichokes. Cut off stems at base and remove small bottom leaves. If desired, trim tips of leaves and cut off about 1 inch from top of artichokes. Stand artichokes upright in deep saucepan large enough to hold snugly. Add ¼ teaspoon salt for each artichoke and 2 to 3 inches boiling water. Add 1 tablespoon lemon juice or vinegar. Cover and boil gently 30 to 45 minutes, or until base of artichoke can be pierced easily with fork. (Add a little more boiling water if needed). Gently spread leaves and remove thistle portion from center of artichoke with metal spoon. Turn artichoke upside down to drain.

Artichokes Genovese

Serves 6

1 can (10¾ ounces) condensed chicken broth
1 cup uncooked rice
½ pound sweet Italian sausage, skinned and chopped
¼ cup minced onion
1½ cups chopped mushrooms
1 package (10 ounces) frozen peas
½ teaspoon Italian herb seasoning
¾ teaspoon salt
⅛ teaspoon freshly ground black pepper
grated Parmesan cheese
6 medium artichokes, prepared as directed above and chilled
¾ cup melted butter or margarine

1. Add enough cold water to broth to make 2 cups; place in heavy saucepan with rice.
2. Bring to a boil; reduce heat to medium-low, stirring once with a fork.
3. Cover and simmer 12 to 14 minutes, or until rice is tender and liquid is absorbed.
4. Cook sausage in skillet until lightly browned; pour off excess fat.
5. Add onion to skillet and sauté until tender.
6. Stir in mushrooms and peas; cook 2 minutes, or until peas are separated.
7. Combine cooked rice, sausage-pea mixture, herb seasoning, salt, pepper and ¼ cup Parmesan cheese; stuff each artichoke with about 1 cup mixture and sprinkle tops with additional cheese.
8. Arrange in shallow baking dish containing 1 inch hot water. Bake, uncovered, in preheated 350° F. oven 30 minutes.
9. Serve with melted butter for dipping leaves.

Artichokes with Vino-Mushroom Sauce

Serves 6

1 can (10¾ ounces) condensed cream of mushroom soup
¼ cup dry white wine
¼ teaspoon thyme leaves, crushed
dash nutmeg
coarsely ground pepper
6 hot cooked artichokes, prepared as directed above

1. Blend together soup, wine, thyme, nutmeg and pepper in saucepan.
2. Bring to boil, stirring constantly.
3. Serve sauce hot with hot artichokes.

Fenella's Carciofini all'Aglio e Prezzemolo
(Artichoke Hearts with Garlic & Parsley)

Serves 4

8 firm, very small artichokes
salted boiling water
½ cup olive oil
2 large cloves garlic, peeled and
chopped fine

½ cup Soave, Frascati or other
Italian white wine
salt to taste
½ cup chopped parsley

1. Trim outer leaves from artichokes and cut off bottoms and tops.
2. Bring 3 inches of lightly boiled salted water to boil in medium saucepan. Add artichokes; cook 5 minutes and drain.
3. Heat olive oil and garlic in another saucepan over low heat, stirring occasionally.
4. Cut each artichoke in half. Place in oil, tossing to coat.
5. Add white wine. Cook over medium heat, stirring until wine has evaporated.
6. Stir in salt to taste and parsley. Stir and cook 5 minutes more.
7. Serve each guest 4 halves.

NOTE: Frozen artichoke hearts can be used. Place in boiling water, let stand 1 minute, drain, and proceed with recipe as directed.

Asparagi alla "Vinaigrette"
(Asparagus Vinaigrette)

Serves 4

1¼ pounds asparagus
½ cup Vinaigrette Dressing

1 tablespoon grated Parmesan cheese
2 cherry tomatoes, sliced (for garnish)
cooked egg yolk, sieved (for garnish)

1. Cook asparagus in 1-inch boiling water until tender, about 8 minutes. Drain.
2. Heat Vinaigrette Dressing in saucepan until hot; pour over asparagus.
3. Sprinkle with cheese; garnish with tomato and egg yolk.

Vinaigrette Dressing
(Salsa Vinaigrette)

Makes 1 cup

¾ cup olive oil
¼ cup red wine vinegar
1 anchovy fillet, mashed (optional)

1 clove garlic, minced
½ teaspoon salt
¼ teaspoon pepper

Shake all ingredients in covered jar; refrigerate.

NOTE: Great to use on greens (mixed) or cold, cooked vegetables for antipasto or salad.

Broccoli all'Aglio
(Sautéed Broccoli with Garlic)

Serves 6

2 pounds broccoli
boiling water
2 cloves garlic, minced

½ cup olive oil
juice of ½ lemon
salt

1. Cut broccoli stalks in half lengthwise.
2. Cook in 1 inch boiling water until just barely tender, about 8 minutes; drain.
3. Sauté garlic in olive oil in skillet 2 minutes.
4. Add broccoli; sauté until tender, 6 to 8 minutes.
5. Sprinkle with lemon and salt. Serve piping hot.

Broccoli Sauté

Serves 4

2 pounds fresh broccoli
½ cup water
¼ cup peanut oil

2 cloves garlic, minced
1 teaspoon salt
⅛ teaspoon pepper

1. Wash broccoli; split ends of large stalks lengthwise into halves or quarters, depending on size.
2. Place in large skillet; sprinkle with water, peanut oil, garlic, salt and pepper.
3. Cover tightly; cook over very low heat 20 to 30 minutes, or until stalks are tender, turning broccoli several times during cooking.

Le Foglie Tenere con Spezie
(Fried Spiced Dandelion Leaves)

Serves 4 to 6

1 pound small spring
  dandelion leaves
2 tablespoons sugar
2 tablespoons white vinegar

1 tablespoon soy sauce
1 teaspoon salt
¼ teaspoon cayenne
1 tablespoon peanut oil

1. Cut leaves into 1 x 1½-inch pieces; wash well.
2. Mix together sugar, vinegar, soy sauce, salt and cayenne in a salad bowl.
3. Gradually mix in oil.
4. Add dandelion leaves; marinate 30 minutes.
5. Drain, but reserve marinade.
6. Place 10-inch skillet over high heat; add additional oil.
7. Reduce heat to medium and add drained dandelion leaves to hot oil. Stir 2 minutes.
8. Remove pan from heat, stir in marinade, mixing well.

Stuffed Eggplant Sicilian

Serves 2

1 medium eggplant, sliced in
  half lengthwise
⅓ cup olive oil
2 cloves garlic, chopped
2 ripe tomatoes, chopped
½ teaspoon basil

1½ cups white bread cubes
¼ cup pine nuts
¼ cup chopped pitted black olives
1 to 2 tablespoons drained capers
salt to taste
pepper to taste

¼ cup grated Parmesan cheese

1. Take meat from eggplant, leaving ½-inch thick shell. (Save shells for stuffing.)
2. Dice meat; sauté in olive oil with garlic 5 minutes.
3. Add tomatoes and basil; cook 5 minutes longer, stirring, until eggplant softens.
4. Stir in bread cubes, pine nuts, olives and capers. Add salt and pepper to taste.
5. Stuff shells. Place stuffed shells in shallow baking pan with ½-inch water. Top with Parmesan cheese.
6. Bake in preheated 400° F. oven 15 to 20 minutes, or until golden brown.

Eggplant Parmigiana

Serves 6 to 8

2 cans (6½ ounces each) chunk
  light tuna
1 medium eggplant
2 eggs, lightly beaten
½ cup flour
½ cup plus 2 tablespoons
  corn oil
1 cup chopped onion
½ cup chopped green pepper
1 clove garlic, minced

1 teaspoon salt
½ teaspoon oregano, crumbled
½ teaspoon sweet basil,
  crumbled
¼ teaspoon rosemary, crumbled
1 can (16 ounces) whole
  tomatoes, drained
½ cup grated Parmesan cheese
1 package (8 ounces) mozzarella
  cheese, shredded

1. Drain tuna and set aside.
2. Slice eggplant into ½-inch slices. Dip each slice in egg and coat with flour.
3. Brown eggplant on both sides in ½ cup oil in a 10-inch skillet. Drain on paper towel.
4. Sauté onion, green pepper and garlic in 2 tablespoons oil until soft.
5. Stir in seasonings, tomatoes and tuna, blending well to break up tomatoes. Simmer 5 minutes.
6. Layer half the browned eggplant slices in bottom of a shallow 2-quart casserole. Sprinkle with half the Parmesan cheese, half the tuna mixture and half the mozzarella cheese. Repeat the layer.
7. Bake in a preheated 350° F. oven 30 minutes, or until bubbly and browned.
8. Cool 10 minutes before serving.

Baked Stuffed Eggplant

Serves 8

2 eggplants (about 1 pound each)
½ cup 100% corn oil margarine
1 cup chopped green pepper
½ cup chopped onion
1 clove garlic, minced
1 can (16 ounces) tomatoes, drained
½ cup chopped parsley
1 teaspoon salt
¼ teaspoon crushed oregano leaves
1 can (3 ounces) sliced mushrooms, drained
1 cup fine dry bread crumbs

1. Cut eggplants in half lengthwise. Scoop out pulp; discard seedy section. Chop remaining pulp.
2. Sauté eggplant in ¼ cup margarine with green pepper, onion and garlic.
3. When onions soften, add tomatoes, parsley, salt, oregano and mushrooms. Cover and simmer 30 minutes.
4. Fill eggplant shells with mixture.
5. Melt remaining margarine. Mix in bread crumbs. Sprinkle on filled shells and press crumbs down in stuffing.
6. Bake in preheated 350° F. oven 30 to 45 minutes, or until tender.

Stuffed Zucchini

Serves 6

3 large zucchini (about 2 pounds)
4 tablespoons 100% corn oil margarine
¼ cup chopped onion
2 tablespoons flour
½ teaspoon salt
dash pepper
1 cup skim milk
1 package (10 ounces) frozen chopped spinach, cooked and drained
⅓ cup fine dry bread crumbs

1. Cook zucchini, covered, in small amount of water until barely tender, about 15 minutes.
2. Drain and cool slightly. Cut in half lengthwise. Scoop out center, leaving a shell ¼-inch thick. Chop pulp and set aside.
3. Melt 2 tablespoons margarine. Add onion and sauté until tender. Blend in flour, salt and pepper.
4. Remove from heat and gradually stir in skim milk.
5. Return to heat and bring mixture to a boil, stirring constantly.
6. Stir in spinach and chopped zucchini pulp.
7. Place zucchini shells in shallow baking dish; fill with spinach mixture.
8. Melt remaining margarine; mix in bread crumbs. Sprinkle over filled shells.
9. Bake in preheated 350° F. oven 20 minutes, or until heated through.

Zucchini con La Salsa
(Squash with Spicy Sauce)

Serves 6

6 medium zucchini
2 tablespoons garlic spread
1 teaspoon seasoned salt

1 package (1½ ounces) spaghetti sauce mix
2 cups Italian plum tomatoes

1. Wash zucchini, trim off ends, and cut in half lengthwise.
2. Brown cut side of zucchini lightly in melted garlic spread for 2 minutes; remove from skillet.
3. Blend spaghetti sauce mix, tomatoes and seasoned salt in skillet; bring to a boil.
4. Add zucchini to sauce, cover, and simmer 15 minutes. Delicious!

Zucchini Vinaigrette

Serves 4 to 6

¼ cup dry white wine
1 package Italian dressing mix
½ cup olive oil
2 tablespoons minced green pepper

2 tablespoons minced fresh parsley
2 minced green onions
3 tablespoons sweet pickle relish
5 to 6 medium-size zucchini

1. Pour wine into pint-size, screw-top jar. Add dressing mix and shake.
2. Add remaining ingredients except zucchini; shake well.
3. Cut ends from zucchini but do not peel. Slice each zucchini into 6 lengthwise strips.
4. Cook zucchini in salted boiling water 3 minutes until slightly crisp.
5. Drain and arrange in shallow dish or pan.
6. Pour vinaigrette sauce over zucchini; marinate several hours or overnight.
7. Serve as a cold vegetable, or on salad greens. Serve alone or garnish with sliced tomatoes.

Cauliflower Marinara

Serves 4 to 6

1 cauliflower head, cored
2 cups Fresh Tomato Sauce
(page 38)

¾ cup grated Parmesan cheese
2 tablespoons chopped fresh
parsley

1. Steam cauliflower until nearly tender.
2. Place on serving platter. Spoon on Tomato Sauce; sprinkle with cheese.
3. Cover with foil and let stand 2 to 3 minutes, until cheese melts.
4. Remove foil, sprinkle with parsley, and serve.

Frito Misto

Serves 6

¾ pound zucchini
¾ pound yellow squash
1 pound eggplant
2 eggs
1 cup water

¾ cup flour
3 tablespoons cornstarch
½ teaspoon baking powder
½ teaspoon salt
peanut oil

1. Cut unpeeled zucchini into ⅜-inch thick diagonal slices.
2. Cut unpeeled yellow squash into 3-inch long pieces and then into sticks, ⅜-inch square.
3. Peel eggplant and cut into ½-inch slices and then into sticks.
4. Mix eggs and water together; gradually add flour, cornstarch, baking powder and salt until smooth. (Add an additional 2 tablespoons flour if batter is too thin. Batter should lightly coat vegetables.)
5. Heat a 1-inch depth of peanut oil in large skillet to 375° F.
6. Dip vegetables in batter and fry until lightly browned, turning once.
7. Drain on paper towels and place on a warm platter. Serve immediately.

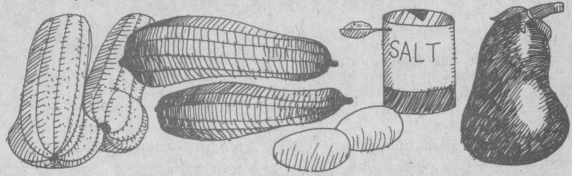

Ratatouilli, Italian Style

Serves 4

2 tablespoons diet imitation
    margarine
1½ cups sliced onions
1 cup sliced green pepper strips
½ teaspoon crushed fresh garlic
1 can (16 ounces) whole peeled
    tomatoes, coarsely chopped

2 cups cubed unpeeled
    eggplant
1½ cups thickly sliced
    unpeeled zucchini
¼ teaspoon thyme leaves
1 bay leaf
dash ground black pepper

1. Melt margarine in Dutch oven over medium heat.
2. Add onions, green pepper and garlic. Sauté, stirring often, until onions are transparent, about 5 minutes.
3. Mix in tomatoes, eggplant, zucchini, thyme, bay leaf and pepper. Cover and simmer over medium low heat, stirring occasionally, until vegetables are tender, about 15 minutes.
4. Remove cover and cook an additional 5 to 10 minutes.

Mushrooms with Tomatoes, Italien

Serves 4 to 6

1 pound very large mushrooms
4 slices bacon
2 small onions, minced
½ teaspoon celery salt
2 teaspoons sugar

5 tomatoes, cut in small pieces
salt to taste
pepper to taste
butter
1 loaf bread

1. Peel and stem mushrooms, using only the caps. (Reserve stems to use in cooking.)
2. Make sauce by dicing bacon very fine and combining with onions. Cook in saucepan until they start to brown.
3. Add seasonings and tomatoes; cover and cook slowly until mixture becomes a mush.
4. Broil or fry mushroom caps in butter.
5. Cut rounds of bread ⅔ inch thick from large loaf of bread. Trim crust as desired. Sauté bread in butter.
6. Place 5 to 6 mushrooms on a slice of bread with stem sides up. Fill caps with tomato mixture.

Italian Stuffed Tomatoes

Serves 4 to 6

4 to 6 large tomatoes
2 tablespoons butter or margarine
½ pound mild Italian sausage, removed from casing and crumbled
1 large onion, chopped

1 clove garlic, minced
¼ teaspoon salt
⅛ teaspoon pepper
½ cup seasoned bread crumbs
¼ cup grated Parmesan cheese
¼ cup chopped parsley

1. Core tomatoes. Scoop out pulp, leaving ¼-inch shell. Chop pulp and set aside. Drain tomatoes on paper towel.
2. Melt butter in medium skillet. Add sausage, onion, garlic, salt and pepper. Cook until meat is browned.
3. Stir in reserved chopped tomato pulp; simmer 5 minutes. Drain.
4. Stir in bread crumbs, Parmesan cheese and parsley. Spoon into tomato shells.
5. Place on a greased baking pan. Bake in preheated 350° F. oven 30 to 35 minutes, or until lightly browned.
6. Sprinkle with additional cheese and chopped parsley, if desired.

Bean Salad Romano

Serves 4

1 head iceberg lettuce
Pesto Dressing
1 can (15 ounces) cannellini beans
   (white kidney beans), drained
½ cup pitted Greek or ripe olives

3 tablespoons freshly grated Parmesan
   cheese
2 tablespoons chopped pimiento
2 tablespoons chopped fresh
   parsley

1. Core and rinse lettuce, drain well; refrigerate in disposable plastic bag or plastic crisper until ready to serve.
2. Prepare Pesto Dressing.
3. Combine beans, olives, 2 tablespoons Parmesan cheese, pimiento and parsley.
4. Pour Pesto Dressing over mixture; toss well to coat beans. Chill several hours, stirring occasionally.
5. At serving time, line 4 individual bowls with lettuce leaves.
6. Shred remaining lettuce to measure 1 quart; add 1 cup to each bowl.
7. Top with beans and their marinade.
8. Sprinkle remaining cheese over beans on each plate.

Pesto Dressing

Makes ½ cup

¼ cup olive oil
¼ cup white wine vinegar
½ teaspoon pressed garlic

1 tablespoon basil
½ teaspoon salt

Combine all ingredients in blender jar. Blend until smooth.

Insalata Palermo
(Palermo Salad)

Serves 4 to 5

1 pound tender young dandelion
   leaves
4 slices bacon, diced
2 tablespoons butter or
   margarine, melted
½ cup heavy cream, sweet or sour

2 eggs, beaten
1 teaspoon salt
½ teaspoon pepper
½ teaspoon paprika
scant tablespoon sugar
1 teaspoon vinegar

1. Wash and dry dandelions (preferably some which have been picked from flowerless stalks). Place in salad bowl.
2. Dice and fry bacon until crisp. Pour bacon pieces and hot drippings over dandelions.
3. Melt butter in skillet from fried bacon. Add remaining ingredients and cook over low heat, stirring constantly until mixture thickens.
4. Pour this piping hot dressing over dandelions and bacon bits and blend thoroughly, tossing up and down with a fork.

Tomato Onion Salad

Serves 6

¼ cup peanut oil
1 tablespoon chopped parsley
1 teaspoon oregano leaves
1 teaspoon salt

¼ teaspoon pepper
3 medium tomatoes, cut in
  small wedges
3 medium onions, thinly sliced

lettuce leaves

1. Combine peanut oil, parsley, oregano, salt and pepper.
2. Marinate tomatoes and onions in oil mixture at least 30 minutes.
3. Serve on lettuce leaves.

Mario's Insalata di Mare
(Italian Seafood Salad)

Serves 8 to 10

½ pound partially-cooked
  conches (large sea snails)
1 pound small squid
1 pint mussels
⅔ cup fine-grade olive oil
¼ cup distilled white vinegar

juice of ½ lemon
¼ teaspoon ground oregano
salt to taste
freshly ground black pepper
  to taste
1 large stalk celery, chopped

chopped fresh parsley (for garnish)

1. Slice conches thinly; set aside.
2. Pull out and discard heads and tentacles from envelope-like bodies of squid. Wash squid carefully, removing speckled skin and insides (including transparent cartilage). Pound to tenderize squid. Boil in enough water to cover for 45 minutes, or until tender. Drain; cut into thin rings.
3. Wash mussels carefully under cold running water. Scrub shells carefully with stiff brush and "debeard" them with sharp knife. Discard any mussels with cracked, broken, or open shells. Place mussels in boiling water in large kettle. Cover and steam 5 minutes, or until shells open. Discard any shells that do not open. Remove mussels from shells and slice; discard shells.
4. Combine mussels with conches and squid. Cover and refrigerate several hours, or until very cold.
5. Combine olive oil, vinegar, lemon juice, oregano, salt and black pepper in screw-top jar. Cover tightly; shake well.
6. Toss seafood mixture with celery; toss with dressing.
7. Serve cold, garnished with parsley.

NOTE: If possible, purchase conches from Italian fish market, where they have been cleaned and partially cooked. They should be cooked about 1 hour. Conches in the shell must be thoroughly scrubbed to remove sand before boiling.

Insalata Italiana
(Italian Salad)

Serves 6

1½ pounds new red potatoes
½ cup Soave white wine
½ cup bottled Italian dressing
¼ cup fresh basil leaves, small or torn, or 2 teaspoons dried basil
½ teaspoon dry tarragon
½ teaspoon salt

1 medium red onion, sliced
1 can (7 ounces) solid white tuna, water-packed, drained
1 can (1 pound 4 ounces) chick peas, drained
3 small tomatoes, quartered
3 hard-cooked eggs, shelled and quartered

¼ pound sliced salami

1. Scrub potatoes under cold running water. Cook in boiling salted water until just tender, about 20 minutes. Cool slightly.
2. Peel and slice into ⅛-inch slices. Place in large bowl, add wine and toss gently. Refrigerate, covered, 2 hours.
3. Combine Italian dressing, basil, tarragon and salt in blender; blend a few seconds until basil is finely chopped.
4. Add onion and tuna to potatoes.
5. Drizzle dressing over mixture, reserving 2 tablespoons.
6. Add reserved dressing to chick peas and toss. Keep chilled until ready to serve.
7. Arrange potato salad and chick peas on large platter; garnish with tomatoes, eggs and salami.

NOTE: If using dried basil, add 2 tablespoons chopped parsley for color along with basil.

Fenella Pearson's Insalata alla Capri
(Salade Capri)

Serves 4

4 firm ripe tomatoes
4 to 6 ounces mozzarella cheese
6 leaves fresh basil

salt
freshly ground black pepper
1 tablespoon wine vinegar

½ cup top-grade olive oil

1. One hour before serving, wash tomatoes and slice.
2. While mozzarella is very cold, slice thinly.
3. Wash basil leaves and tear into small pieces.
4. Place tomatoes, cheese and basil in serving bowl. Sprinkle with salt, grind some pepper over it, and sprinkle with vinegar. Toss.
5. Sprinkle with olive oil and gently toss again.

NOTE: An interesting side dish, this also may be served as a main course salad. Use only fresh basil!

Roman Garden Salad

Serves 8 to 10

1 package (10 ounces) frozen
  Italian cut green beans
½ cup olive oil
¼ cup corn oil
½ cup red wine vinegar
1 teaspoon dried sweet basil,
  crumbled
¼ teaspoon dried thyme,
  crumbled

⅛ teaspoon garlic powder
½ teaspoon salt
dash ground black pepper
1 small red onion, thinly sliced
2 cups cauliflowerets
1 fresh zucchini, thinly sliced
3 cups fresh mushrooms, sliced
crisp salad greens
1 large ripe tomato

1. Cook beans as directed.
2. Blend together olive oil, corn oil, vinegar, basil, thyme, garlic powder, salt and pepper.
3. Separate onion into rings and cauliflowerets into bite-size pieces.
4. Place onion rings in large glass serving bowl. Spoon 3 tablespoons dressing over onions.
5. Layer all zucchini slices, cauliflowerets, green beans and mushrooms, spooning dressing over each layer. Top with remaining dressing.
6. Cover and chill 1 to 4 hours.
7. Arrange crisp salad greens on serving plates. Slice tomato, arrange on greens.
8. Serve marinated vegetables in large bowl and let each person spoon vegetables onto tomato.

Insalata Con Crema
(Dandelion Salad in Cream)

Serves 4 to 5

½ pound freshly picked young
  dandelion leaves
5 young dandelion roots
1 cup dairy sour cream

2 teaspoons fresh lemon juice
2 teaspoons sugar
1 teaspoon salt
1 teaspoon pepper (less, if desired)

1. Clean greens under running water, making certain all sand is washed away; shred to fork-size pieces.
2. Scrub roots, scrape well, and slice into ¼-inch rounds; add roots to greens and chill.
3. Combine sour cream, lemon juice, sugar, salt and pepper in separate bowl; mix well.
4. Just before serving, take greens from refrigerator and add enough dressing to moisten greens.

NOTE: Dandelions are a favorite with Italians. When they begin popping up all over your lawn, scoop them up with a trowel and wash carefully before crisping like any other greens. Dandelions taste different from anything you've ever had! They are exceptionally high in vitamin A and a secondary source of calcium and iron. Great with veal!

Pizza

Makes about 6 pounds dough

2 packages active dry yeast
1 teaspoon sugar
¼ cup warm water (100° F.)
4 cups hot water

⅓ cup olive oil
1 teaspoon salt
1½ cups nonfat dry milk powder
about 12 cups unbleached white flour (amount varies)

To Make Dough

1. Stir together yeast, sugar and ¼ cup warm water in warm quart-size mixing bowl. Set aside to proof. (Yeast will start working quickly if it is good.)
2. Stir into large warm mixing bowl: hot water, oil, salt, milk and 6 cups flour.
3. Add yeast mixture; stir in 3 additional cups flour slowly. Continue to add flour gradually, stirring very vigorously.
4. When dough is too stiff to stir, dump out on a lightly floured board and knead until smooth and elastic, 10 to 15 minutes, adding just enough flour to keep dough from sticking. (The 12-cup estimate of flour can vary greatly. You can use half whole wheat flour, but dough will not be as elastic.)
5. Cut into ½-pound pieces for individual pizzas or calzoni. Form into balls, rub with additional olive oil, and allow to rise in warm place on a plate or a pan large enough so they don't touch and stick together. Let dough rise until double in bulk.

To Assemble

1. Place ball of risen dough on floured board.
2. Pound flat with hands, being careful to keep round shape. (Use rolling pin if needed.) Dough should be evenly thin and as big around as your dinner plates.
3. Top with desired ingredients (mushrooms, mozzarella cheese, onions, peppers, sliced tomatoes, sliced salami, Parmesan cheese, pizza sauce, etc.).
4. Place on oiled pan or baking sheet in preheated 450° F. oven; bake until crust is golden brown on sides and bottom and toppings are heated through, 8 to 18 minutes, depending on your oven.

Pizza Sauce

Makes enough for 3 or 4 large pizzas or
12 individual calzoni

1 bulb fresh garlic
⅓ cup olive oil
1 can (28 ounces) peeled Italian
 tomatoes, diced, or 2 pounds fresh
 peeled tomatoes, diced

1 can (29 ounces) heavy tomato
 purée
1½ tablespoons dry whole basil
1½ tablespoons dry whole oregano
½ teaspoon salt
1 teaspoon crushed hot red pepper

1. Separate and clean cloves of garlic. Slice them thinly, crosswise.
2. Heat garlic in olive oil in large kettle until garlic is sizzling but not brown.
3. Pour tomatoes and tomato purée into kettle; stir in basil, oregano, salt, and red pepper. Simmer 15 minutes, stirring often.
4. Allow to cool.

Calzoni

Pizza dough (page 84)
pizza sauce, homemade or prepared

Cheeses:
  whole-milk mozzarella
  ricotta
  Bel Paese
  Parmesan
  Romano

Other fillings:
  ham (prosciutto)
    or sausage
  onions and/or mushrooms
    sautéed with garlic
  marinated artichoke hearts
    or black olives

1. Take ½-pound ball of risen dough; place on floured board. Pound flat with hand, being careful to retain round shape. (Use rolling pin if needed.) Dough should be evenly thin and as big around as a dinner plate.
2. Spread sauce over whole dough, except for 1-inch border around edge.
3. Put grated cheeses and other fillings on half of sauced area. Use any combination you like, but be careful not to pile too much on. Fold other side of dough over fillings; seal edges by pressing borders firmly with fingers.
4. Rub a little olive oil over top of each calzoni. Put 1 tablespoon sauce or cheese on top as decoration, or to denote what filling is inside.
5. Bake on oiled pan or baking sheet in preheated 450° F. oven until crust is golden on sides and bottom, 8 to 18 minutes, depending on your oven.

NOTE: Each calzoni will make a meal. Packs well to take along on a picnic.

Tony's Focaccia
(Italian Snack)

Serves 10

1 package (13¾ ounces) hot
  roll mix
1 cup wheat germ, regular
1 cup water

½ cup fine-grade olive oil
½ cup grated Romano cheese
1 clove garlic, minced
2 teaspoons oregano, crumbled

1 teaspoon basil, crumbled

1. Mix dry portion of hot roll mix with ¾ cup wheat germ; prepare dough according to package directions, increasing water from ¾ to 1 cup.
2. Let dough rise; knead as directed.
3. Roll out on lightly floured board to form a 15 x 1-inch rectangle; transfer to greased baking sheet. Press thumbs into dough at 1-inch intervals.
4. Combine oil, cheese, garlic, oregano and basil; spread over dough and sprinkle with remaining wheat germ.
5. Let rise in warm place, free from drafts, about 45 minutes, or until doubled.
6. Bake in preheated 450° F. oven 10 to 12 minutes, or until edges are nicely browned.
7. Cut into squares or rectangles and serve piping hot. Great served with a glass of your favorite vino for a light snack.

Italian Egg Nest Coffee Cake

Makes 1 coffee cake

about 3 cups unsifted flour
½ cup sugar
¾ teaspoon salt
1 package active dry yeast
¾ cup plus 2 tablespoons milk
¼ cup plus 2 teaspoons 100% corn
  oil margarine, softened
1 egg (at room temperature)
2 tablespoons melted margarine

¾ teaspoon cinnamon
⅛ teaspoon nutmeg
½ cup golden raisins
1½ cups confectioner's sugar
1 tablespoon light corn syrup
1 teaspoon lemon extract
food coloring
milk
½ cup flaked coconut

1. Mix together 2¼ cups flour, ¼ cup sugar, salt and yeast in a small mixing bowl.
2. Heat ¾ cup milk and ¼ cup margarine in saucepan over low heat until very warm, 120° F. - 130° F. (Margarine does not have to melt.)
3. Gradually add heated mixture to dry ingredients; beat 2 minutes at medium speed of electric mixer, scraping bowl occasionally.
4. Add egg and ½ cup flour, or enough flour to make a thick batter. Beat at high speed 2 minutes, scraping bowl occasionally.
5. Stir in enough additional flour to make a soft dough.
6. Turn onto lightly floured board; knead until smooth and elastic, 8 to 10 minutes.
7. Place in greased bowl, turning to grease top. Cover; let rise in warm place, free from draft, until doubled in bulk, about 1¼ hours.
8. Punch down dough; turn out onto lightly floured board. Form dough into a large ball.
9. Tear off 5 pieces about the size of small eggs. Form into smooth egg shapes.
10. Roll remaining dough into an 18 x 7-inch rectangle. Brush lightly with melted margarine.
11. Combine remaining sugar, cinnamon, nutmeg, and raisins; sprinkle over dough.
12. Roll up from long side as for jelly roll. Seal edges firmly.
13. Place sealed edge down in circle on greased baking sheet. Seal ends together firmly.
14. Slash top of ring at 2-inch intervals. Place dough eggs inside ring.
15. Cover; let rise in warm place, free from draft, until doubled in bulk, about 1 hour.
16. Bake in preheated 350° F. oven 20 minutes, or until done.
17. Remove from baking sheet; cool on wire rack.
18. Meanwhile, combine confectioners' sugar, remaining 2 tablespoons milk, corn syrup, remaining 2 tablespoons softened margarine and lemon extract. Beat until smooth.
19. Frost ring, using ½ of frosting.
20. Dilute food coloring with few drops of milk (prepare 5 colors).
21. Use a few drops of diluted green to tint half the coconut, leaving other half white. Sprinkle green and white coconut over ring.
22. Mix small amounts of remaining frosting with other diluted colors. Frost each egg a different color.

NOTE: In Italy, festive Easter breads are baked with colored eggs nested in the dough. This recipe is an interesting variation of the traditional Italian egg bread. The rich sweet dough is prepared by the "rapidmix method" (yeast is added to some of the dry ingredients), eliminating dissolving yeast in warm water. In addition, this method calls for initial beating with an electirc mixer that prevents lumping and makes the dough easier to handle.

Panettone

Makes 2 loaves

2 packages active dry yeast
¼ cup lukewarm water
¾ cup boiling water
¼ pound butter, softened
½ cup sugar
2 teaspoons salt
4 eggs, beaten
2 teaspoons anise extract

about 6 cups sifted all-purpose
 flour
1 cup seedless golden raisins
⅓ cup candied cherries, halved
⅓ cup candied orange or lemon
 peel, chopped
⅓ cup chopped candied citron
melted butter

1. Soften yeast in lukewarm water in small bowl; set aside.
2. Pour boiling water over butter, sugar and salt in large mixing bowl. Stir until butter melts and sugar dissolves. Cool to lukewarm.
3. Add eggs and anise; beat until well blended.
4. Stir in half the flour; add yeast mixture and stir. Add enough remaining flour to form a soft dough. Turn out on lightly floured board; knead until smooth and elastic.
5. Put into greased bowl, turn to grease top of dough. Cover with cloth; let rise in warm place, free from drafts, until double in bulk, about 2 hours.
6. When dough has doubled, punch down and knead in fruits.
7. Shape into 2 loaves. Place on greased baking sheets; brush with melted butter.
8. Let rise until double in bulk, about 1 hour. With sharp knife, cut slashes on top.
9. Bake in preheated 350° F. oven 50 minutes, or until done. Brush again with melted butter. Cool on wire racks.

Italian Easter Fig Buns

Makes 12 buns

1½ cups finely chopped dried
 figs (in grinder or food processor)
¾ cup water
⅓ cup Amaretto liqueur
¾ cup coarsely chopped walnuts
4 cups biscuit mix
colored sprinkles

2 eggs
⅓ cup sugar
¾ cup milk
grated rind of 1 lemon
1½ cups confectioners' sugar
milk

1. Combine figs, water, Amaretto and nuts in saucepan. Cook, stirring occasionally, until mixture is thick and jam-like. Set aside.
2. Combine biscuit mix, eggs, sugar, milk and lemon rind in mixing bowl.
3. Turn dough out on a heavily floured board; knead a few times into a smooth ball.
4. Divide dough into 12 pieces. Flatten each piece into a 3-inch round on a greased cookie sheet, 2 inches apart.
5. Press with floured fingers firmly in center to make a deep depression; fill center with a generous amount of fig filling.
6. Bake in preheated 375° F. oven 15 to 20 minutes, or until golden. Cool.
7. Mix confectioners' sugar with additional milk, enough to make mixture the consistency of thick sour cream. Spoon over dough part of buns and sprinkle with colored sprinkles.

Almond Cassata

Serves 4 to 6

1 small pound cake (10 ounces)
8 ounces ricotta cheese
2 tablespoons granulated sugar
1 tablespoon light cream
½ teaspoon orange extract
½ cup chopped natural almonds, toasted

2 tablespoons mixed candied fruit, finely chopped
1 package (6 ounces) real semi-sweet chocolate pieces
2 tablespoons water
¼ cup butter or margarine

1. If top of pound cake is rounded, slice off top to make level, using sharp serrated knife. Cut cake horizontally to make 3 equal layers.
2. Combine ricotta cheese, sugar, cream and orange extract in small bowl; beat with electric mixer until smooth.
3. Add ¼ cup almonds, candied fruit and 2 tablespoons chocolate pieces, finely chopped.
4. Center bottom layer of cake on flat plate; spread with half of ricotta mixture.
5. Arrange second layer on top and spread with remaining ricotta mixture.
6. Gently spread third layer in place.
7. Refrigerate 2 hours, or until ricotta mixture is firm.
8. Melt remaining chocolate pieces with water in small heavy saucepan over low heat. Stir until chocolate is completely melted.
9. Remove from heat, stir in butter, one tablespoon at a time. Continue stirring until mixture is smooth.
10. Refrigerate ½ hour until frosting is of spreading consistency.
11. With a spatula, spread frosting thinly on top and sides of cake, swirling to decorate. Garnish with remaining almonds. Chill at least ½ hour before slicing.

Cassata

one pound cake (16 ounces)
¾ cup plus 1½ teaspoons Cointreau, divided
15 ounces ricotta cheese
1 pound plus ½ cup confectioners' sugar, divided

1 cup candied fruit, diced
4 ounces unsweetened chocolate
½ cup butter
1 teaspoon pure vanilla extract

1. Slice pound cake into 3 layers. Brush ¼ cup Cointreau on sides of layers.
2. Mix together ricotta cheese, ½ cup confectioners' sugar, 1½ teaspoons Cointreau and diced candied fruit pieces; spread mixture between layers.
3. Melt chocolate and butter over low heat; remove from heat.
4. Stir in ½ cup Cointreau and vanilla.
5. Gradually add about 1 pound sifted confectioners' sugar; beat until smooth.
6. Chill a few minutes to thicken, if needed.
7. Frost in thin layer. With pastry bag, use remainder of frosting to decorate.

Classic Italian Cheesecake

Makes 1 nine-inch cake

For the Crust

1¼ cups sifted all-purpose
flour
¼ cup sugar
½ teaspoon salt

½ teaspoon grated lemon rind
½ cup sweet butter
1 egg yolk
2 tablespoons Liquore Galliano

1. Mix together flour, sugar, salt and lemon rind in mixing bowl.
2. Cut in butter until mixture resembles coarse meal.
3. Mix in egg yok and liquore until pastry is blended.
4. Press pastry over bottom and up sides (1¾ inches) of a 9-inch spring-form pan.
5. Bake in preheated 350° F. oven 15 minutes, or until dry, but not browned.

For the Filling

2 containers (15 ounces each)
ricotta or cottage cheese
4 eggs
½ cup sugar
¼ cup all-purpose flour

¼ cup Liquore Galliano
2 tablespoons golden raisins
2 tablespoons candied orange
or lemon peel, finely
grated

1. Blend together cheese, eggs, sugar and flour in mixing bowl.
2. Stir in liquore, raisins and grated peel.
3. Pour filling into crust in pan. Bake in preheated 325° F. oven 1 hour, or until cake tests done.
4. Release cake from spring-form pan and cool on rack.

Demitasse Blueberry Tortoni

Serves 6

1 cup heavy cream
¼ cup confectioner's sugar
1 teaspoon pure vanilla
extract

1 teaspoon rum flavoring
1 cup fresh or dry-pack
frozen blueberries, rinsed
and drained

⅓ cup crisp crumbled macaroons

1. Combine cream, sugar, vanilla and rum flavoring in bowl. Whip until stiff.
2. Fold in blueberries and ¼ cup crumbs.
3. Pile mixture into demitasse cups. Sprinkle with remaining crumbs and decorate with additional blueberries.
4. Freeze until firm; wrap and store until needed. Serve frozen in demitasse cups set on saucers.

Amaretti
(Almond Cookies)

Makes about 3 dozen cookies

2 cups blanched almonds
1 cup sugar
1 teaspoon almond extract

2 egg whites, beaten
until stiff
confectioners' sugar

1. Grind almonds finely.
2. Spread on baking sheet, allowing to dry several hours.
3. Combine almonds, sugar and almond extract.
4. Fold in beaten egg whites; blend gently.
5. Drop batter by teaspoons onto greased, floured cookie sheets, allowing 2 inches between cookies. Sprinkle with confectioners' sugar.
6. Allow cookies to stand, uncovered, at room temperature to dry before baking (about 1 hour).
7. Bake in preheated 325° F. oven 15 minutes, or until golden.
8. Cool on cookie sheets several minutes before removing to rack.

NOTE: These cookies can be frozen.

Castagne
(Chestnuts with Whipped Cream)

Serves 4

1 pound raw chestnuts
about 1½ cups water
dash of salt
⅓ cup confectioners' sugar

¾ cup heavy cream
1 teaspoon pure vanilla
extract or ½ teaspoon
ground nutmeg

1. Cook chestnuts in water to cover for 15 to 20 minutes. Drain, peel and skin chestnuts.
2. Put parboiled chestnuts in saucepan with water. Add salt, cover tightly, and cook until soft.
3. Drain and mash chestnuts until smooth.
4. Add sugar.
5. Whip cream until stiff. Reserve ⅓ cup whipped cream for garnish and add remainder to chestnuts.
6. Add vanilla or nutmeg.
7. Chill at least 6 hours.
8. Serve in glass dishes; garnish with dollop of whipped cream.

Granita di Limone
(Lemon Ice)

Serves 8

1½ cups water
1 cup sugar
½ cup Soave wine

grated rind of 4 lemons
¾ to 1 cup fresh lemon
juice

1. Heat water and sugar to a boil in saucepan; boil 3 minutes.
2. Cool. Mix all the ingredients together.
3. Freeze in 9-inch pan until firm, about 3 hours.

NOTE: A favorite sweet with Italians! Great in other flavors too, including tangerine, orange or raspberry.

Zabaglione

Serves 4

6 large egg yolks

⅓ cup sugar
⅓ cup Marsala or dry sherry

1. Heat egg yolks in top of double boiler, beating until thick.
2. Gradually add sugar, continuing to beat until thick and foamy. Be careful that water in lower part of double boiler does **not** touch top pan!
3. Add Marsala slowly, beating continuously until custard becomes thick and lemon-colored.
4. Pour into sherbet glasses. Serve immediately. Rich and wonderful!

Marsala Poached Pears

Serves 4

¾ cup sugar
⅔ cup water

½ cup sweet Marsala wine
4 ripe pears

whipped cream (optional garnish)

1. Combine sugar, water and wine in medium saucepan. Bring to a boil over medium high heat, stirring to dissolve sugar.
2. Reduce heat to low. Set pears in simmering liquid. Cover and cook until tender, 15 to 20 minutes.
3. Remove pears from pan with slotted spoon and chill.
4. Increase heat to medium-high; reduce liquid in pan until thickened to syrup consistency.
5. Chill sauce.
6. Place each pear in a serving dish. Spoon 2 tablespoons sauce around each pear. Garnish with whipped cream, if desired.

Tagliatelle con le Mele Fiorentina
(Noodle Dessert Florentine)

Serves 6

6 ounces fine or medium noodles
¼ cup butter or margarine,
  melted
3 cups applesauce
2 eggs

¾ cup brown sugar
1 teaspoon vanilla
¾ teaspoon cinnamon
1 cup raisins
½ cup chopped almonds
whipped cream

1. Cook noodles according to package directions. Drain.
2. Toss noodles with melted butter.
3. Combine remaining ingredients except whipped cream. Fold mixture into noodles.
4. Pour into a buttered 8-inch square pan. Bake in preheated 375° F. oven 45 minutes.
5. Serve warm, topped with whipped cream.

Sicilian Torta de Crema

Serves 8 to 10

2 quarts milk
⅔ cup cornstarch
¾ cup sugar
grated peel from 2 large lemons

1 pound cake (1 pound) cut into
  8 slices
1 cup strong coffee
1 bar (8 ounces) milk chocolate, grated

1. Combine milk, cornstarch, sugar and lemon peel in saucepan. Cook, stirring, over low heat until thick.
2. Spoon half of thickened cream sauce into 13 x 9-inch glass dish. Top with cake slices.
3. Spoon 2 tablespoons coffee over each cake slice. Spread remaining cream on top.
4. Refrigerate several hours, or until very cold.
5. Sprinkle grated chocolate over top. Serve at once.

Cappucino

Serves 1

½ teaspoon sugar
½ teaspoon cocoa powder
2½ ounces strong black coffee

2½ ounces half-and-half
1½ ounces brandy
whipped cream

1. Combine sugar and cocoa.
2. Mix with coffee and half-and-half in 8-ounce serving glass.
3. Add brandy and top with whipped cream.

Italian Cherry-Chocolate Tortoni

Serves 10

2 egg whites
4 tablespoons sugar
3 tablespoons cocoa
1 jar (12 ounces)
  maraschino cherries

½ cup sliced almonds
1 quart vanilla ice cream,
  softened
½ cup heavy cream

1. Beat egg whites until foamy.
2. Gradually beat in 3 tablespoons sugar, continuing to beat until stiff peaks form.
3. Beat in cocoa.
4. Drain cherries, reserving 10 cherries for garnish. Chop remaining cherries.
5. Fold cherries and almonds into softened ice cream.
6. Carefully fold beaten egg whites into ice cream.
7. Fill paper soufflé cups. Freeze until firm, or overnight.
8. To serve, beat cream and remaining sugar together until stiff. Place dollop of sweetened cream on each tortoni. Garnish with a cherry.

NOTE: *To store longer, wrap each tortoni separately in plastic wrap and return to freezer.*

Italian Torta

Serves 10

6 large apples, preferably
  Red Delicious
½ lemon rind, grated
12 macaroon cookies, crushed
¾ cup sugar
pinch salt
2 tablespoons all-purpose flour
½ teaspoon nutmeg

4 eggs, beaten slightly
¼ teaspoon almond extract
4 teaspoons Angostura aromatic
  bitters
¾ cup milk
1 teaspoon butter, softened
split blanched almonds
maraschino cherries

whipped cream (optional)

1. Peel and grate apples.
2. Add lemon rind, macaroon crumbs, sugar, salt, flour, nutmeg, eggs, almond extract and Angostura aromatic bitters. Mix together thoroughly.
3. Stir in milk; blend well.
4. Pour into well-greased 8-inch baking dish. Dot top with butter.
5. Bake in preheated 325° F. oven 2 hours, or until knife inserted in center comes out clean. (Consistency should be that of a firm pudding.)
6. Decorate with almonds and cherries. Chill well. Serve plain or with whipped cream.

Cannoli Pie

Serves 6 to 8

1½ pounds ricotta cheese
1½ cups confectioners' sugar
3 tablespoons heavy cream
12 maraschino cherries, quartered
2 ounces baker's sweet chocolate,
   coarsely grated

2 ounces slivered almonds
1 commercially prepared
   chocolate crust
grated baker's sweet chocolate
   (optional garnish)

1. Combine ricotta cheese, confectioners' sugar and heavy cream in large mixing bowl; blend well until smooth and creamy.
2. Add cherries, 2 ounces chocolate and almonds; stir to blend in.
3. Pour into prepared crust. Decorate with sprinkling of grated chocolate, if desired.
4. Cover with foil and freeze 3 hours before serving. (If pie becomes solid, allow to soften slightly before serving.)

NOTE: A classic Italian dessert.

Mama Leone's Blueberry Tortoni

Serves 8

½ cup sugar
¼ cup water
3 egg yolks
⅔ cup almond paste
3 tablespoons pineapple juice
   or light cream

dash salt
1½ cup heavy cream, whipped
1 cup fresh blueberries, rinsed
   and drained, or 1 cup frozen
   dry-pack blueberries
½ cup toasted chopped almonds

1. Combine sugar and water in a saucepan. Bring to a boil until candy thermometer registers 240° F., or until a few drops dropped into cold water form a soft ball.
2. Beat egg yolks until thick and lemon colored.
3. Gradually beat hot syrup into yolks until mixture is very thick.
4. Gradually beat in almond paste, pineapple juice and salt.
5. Fold in heavy cream and blueberries.
6. Spoon mixture into 4-ounce soufflé cups. Decorate top with a few blueberries and a sprinkle of toasted almonds.
7. Freeze until firm. When frozen hard, overwrap to prevent crystalling. Serve frozen.

Classic Macedoine of Fruit

Serves 8

1 ripe pineapple, cut in spears
2 grapefruits, sectioned
4 oranges, sectioned
2 apples, unpeeled and sliced
2 pears, unpeeled and sliced

black and white grapes, seeded
 and halved
1¼ cups Liquore Galliano
2 tablespoons orange juice
1 cup red currant jelly

1. Combine fruit in large shallow bowl.
2. Stir in 1 cup liquore. Cover and chill 4 hours, or overnight.
3. Drain, reserving liquid for sauce or compotes.
4. Combine remaining liquore, orange juice and jelly in saucepan; heat to melt jelly.
5. Brush mixture thickly on fruit.

Italian Raisin Cake

Serves 10 to 12

1 pound seedless raisins
2 cups water
1 teaspoon baking soda
½ cup soft butter
1½ cups sugar
3 large eggs

1 teaspoon salt
½ teaspoon ground cloves
½ teaspoon ground nutmeg
2 teaspoons ground cinnamon
3 cups cake flour
2 cups chopped walnuts

1. Plump raisins by cooking them in water 10 minutes; strain and reserve 1 cup liquid.
2. Add baking soda to reserved raisin liquid; set aside.
3. Cream together butter, sugar, eggs, salt and spices until fluffy.
4. Add flour and liquid alternately, beating well after each addition.
5. Stir in raisins and nuts; beat thoroughly.
6. Pour into a well-greased 1-inch tube pan; bake in preheated 325° F. oven 1½ hours, or until a toothpick inserted in center comes out clean.
7. Cool on wire rack before removing from pan.

Italian Tangerine Ice

Makes 2 quarts

½ cup sugar
peel from 2 tangerines
1 teaspoon unflavored gelatin

1½ cups water
juice and pulp of 3 tangerines
½ cup fresh orange juice

1½ teaspoons fresh lemon juice

1. Combine sugar, peel, gelatin and water in saucepan; stir until sugar is dissolved. Boil 3 minutes; cool.
2. Add tangerine juice and pulp, orange and lemon juices; press through sieve, then freeze in tray until mixture is snowy and frothy.
3. Serve in tall glasses. Delightful on a hot summer day.

NOTE: This is similar to the Italian ice served from pushcarts in Italian neighborhoods.

Biscuit Tortoni

Serves 8

⅓ cup toasted almonds
  or pine nuts
⅓ cup sugar

2 tablespoons water
2 tablespoons dry sherry
2 egg yolks

1 cup heavy cream, whipped

1. Put nuts into container of electric blender. Cover and blend on high speed 4 to 5 seconds.
2. Turn out on wax paper; set aside.
3. Combine sugar and water in small saucepan; boil 3 minutes.
4. Put sherry and egg yolks in blender container. Cover; turn motor on high for a few seconds until thick and creamy.
5. Remove cover and gradually add syrup.
6. Fold sherry-yolk mixture into whipped cream.
7. Arrange 8 paper soufflé liners in muffin tin or refrigerator tray. Spoon tortoni mixture into cups. Sprinkle tops with ground nuts. Freeze 2 to 3 hours, or until frozen.

Almond Strawberry Zabaglione

Serves 4

2⅔ cups sliced strawberries
½ cup sliced natural almonds,
  toasted

6 egg yolks
⅔ cup granulated sugar
½ cup Marsala wine or dry sherry

4 whole strawberries (for garnish)

1. Place ⅓ cup sliced strawberries in bottom of each serving dish.
2. Sprinkle 1 tablespoon almonds over berries in each dish.
3. Whip egg yolks with sugar in top of double boiler.
4. Add Marsala, stirring constantly.
5. Set double boiler over cold water and cook mixture over medium heat, stirring constantly, until sauce is thick and creamy.
6. Spoon sauce over fruit and almonds.
7. Arrange ⅓ cup strawberry slices over sauce in each dish. Sprinkle each with remaining almonds. Garnish with whole strawberries.

HL-1M/D8000-2/1`/3